DK EYEW

TO

CAPE TOWN &
THE WINELANDS

PHILIP BRIGGS

Top 10 Cape Town and the Winelands Highlights

The Top 10 of Everything

CONTENTS

Cape Town and the Winelands Area by Area

Streetsmart

Within each Top 10 list in this book, no hierarchy of quality or popularity is implied. All 10 are, in the editor's opinion, of roughly equal merit.

Front cover and spine *Table Mountain and Lion's Head as seen from Signal Hill*
Back cover *Brightly coloured beach huts on Muizenberg beach, False Bay*
Title page *Kirstenbosch National Botanical Garden, with Table Mountain in the background*

Welcome to
Cape Town and the Winelands

Modern visitors would surely agree with Sir Francis Drake's description of the region as "the fairest Cape in the whole circumference of the earth". Perched at the foot of Africa, Cape Town's golden beaches, wild forests and rugged peaks melt into rolling, vine-covered slopes. With Eyewitness Top 10 Cape Town and the Winelands, it's yours to explore.

Cape Town is a haven for outdoor enthusiasts: you can hike the footpaths on **Table Mountain**, picnic on the lawns at **Kirstenbosch**, don a wetsuit and learn to surf or people-watch at a pavement café over a glass of local wine. Within an hour's drive there are hundreds of wine estates, where you can sample vintages in centuries-old manor houses or bold modern buildings decked out with local art.

Food and drink are just as important as natural beauty in the so-called Mother City, whether you're looking for Cape Malay *bobotie* and a bottle of craft beer in **Bo-Kaap** or fine dining and a flight of wines at a **Stellenbosch** estate. Festivals are also a way of life here, epitomized by flamboyant parades such as **Kaapse Klopse**, the colourful New Year carnival.

Whether you're visiting for a weekend or a week or longer, our Top 10 guide is designed to bring together the best of everything that Cape Town and the Winelands have to offer, from the cafés, shops and museums of the **V&A Waterfront** to the windswept coves of the **Cape of Good Hope**. The guide gives you tips throughout, from seeking out what's free to avoiding the crowds, plus six easy-to-follow itineraries designed to tie together a clutch of sights in a short space of time. Add inspiring photography and detailed maps, and you've got the essential pocket-sized travel companion. **Enjoy the book, and enjoy Cape Town and the Winelands.**

Clockwise from top: **View of the Lion's Head from Table Mountain**; African penguin on Boulders Beach; V&A Waterfront, Cape Town; wine estate near Franschhoek; a protea, the national flower, at Kirstenbosch National Botanical Garden; beach huts at Muizenberg; guards during the Key Ceremony at the Castle of Good Hope

Exploring Cape Town and the Winelands

Cape Town and its glorious surrounds offer something for every type of traveller, from the hardy hiker to the discerning gourmet. However long your stay, you'll want to make the most of your time, so here are two sightseeing itineraries to help you get the very best out of your visit to Cape Town and the Winelands.

Table Mountain's Upper Cableway viewpoint offers breathtaking vistas.

Two Days in Cape Town

Day ❶
MORNING
Take the cable car to the top of **Table Mountain** *(see pp22–3)* and allow an hour or so to admire the views.
AFTERNOON
Wander the **Company's Garden** *(see pp12–13)* and visit the fascinating Iziko Slave Lodge. Drop in to the poignant **District Six Museum** *(see pp18–19)* and end your day with an afternoon tea at the **Mount Nelson** *(see p114)*.

Day ❷
MORNING
Get an early start for the drive to **Cape Point** *(see pp32–3)* and have breakfast at the **Two Oceans Restaurant** *(see p89)*. Then take the scenic drive to **Simon's Town** *(see pp30–31)* to see the colony of African penguins.

AFTERNOON
Enjoy lunch and wine tasting at the historic **Groot Constantia** *(see pp28–9)*. Complete your day with a stroll through the **Kirstenbosch National Botanical Garden** *(see pp26–7)* and high tea in the Tea Room Restaurant.

Seven Days in Cape Town and the Winelands

Day ❶
Start with a trip to the top of **Table Mountain** *(see pp22–3)*. Later, have lunch on trendy Bree Street, haggle for curios at **Greenmarket Square** *(see p67)* and follow the Fan Walk to **Green Point Urban Park** *(see p70)*.

Day ❷
Book ahead for the boat trip to **Robben Island** *(see pp16–17)* and take a fascinating guided tour.

Key
— Two-day itinerary
— Seven-day itinerary

Paarl

Boschendal

Stellenbosch

Franschhoek

Lanzerac

Spier

0 kilometres 10

0 miles 10

Cape Town

from Robben Island

V&A Waterfront

BOAT

Green Point Urban Park

Two Oceans Aquarium

Bree Street

Greenmarket Square

Iziko Slave Lodge

Castle of Good Hope

Company's Garden

District Six Museum

Mount Nelson

Table Mountain

0 km 1

0 miles 1

and explore the park's many museums. Reward yourself with a decadent high tea at the **Mount Nelson** (see p114).

Day ❺
Drive out to Stellenbosch (see pp34–5) to indulge in some wine tasting at gorgeous Lanzerac or family-friendly **Spier** (see p57). Book ahead for lunch at one of the estates. Sip wine (unless you are the driver) under the trees at **Boschendal** (see p92), then make your way to pretty **Franschhoek** (see pp36–7) and spend the rest of the day and evening exploring the galleries and restaurants of the main street.

Day ❻
Enjoy a French-themed breakfast in Franschhoek, then head to **Paarl** (see p92) and visit Spice Route to taste artisanal produce. Afterwards, head back to Cape Town to spend some time enjoying the beautiful beaches of **Camps Bay** and **Clifton** (see p51).

Day ❼
Try a surfing class in **Muizenberg** (see p50) or browse the eclectic shops of **Kalk Bay** (see p87). Head to the Constantia wineries for lunch, and visit **Groot Constantia** (see pp28–9) or **Buitenverwachting** (see p80) for a little wine tasting. Then take a leisurely stroll or hike through the magnificent **Kirstenbosch National Botanical Garden** (see pp26–7).

Enjoy a seafood lunch at the **V&A Waterfront** (see pp14–15) followed by a visit to the aquarium, a bit of shopping and watching street performers.

Day ❸
Head to **Hout Bay** (see p86) for breakfast, ideally on a weekend when the market is operating. Follow stunning **Chapman's Peak Drive** (see p86) then explore the windswept **Cape of Good Hope** (see pp22–3). Pay an afternoon visit to the delightful penguin colony at Boulders Beach and then dine at the water's edge in **Simon's Town** (see pp30–31).

Day ❹
Explore the **Castle of Good Hope** (see pp20–21), South Africa's oldest building, then brush up on more recent history at the **District Six Museum** (see pp18–19). Enjoy a picnic in the **Company's Garden** (see pp12–13),

Stellenbosch is the lovely historic capital of the lush Winelands.

Top 10 Cape Town and the Winelands Highlights

View from Cape Point, overlooking
the Cape of Good Hope

TOP 10 Cape Town and the Winelands Highlights

Cape Town, set between the imperious heights of Table Mountain and the blue depths of the Atlantic, offers a Mediterranean climate, a vibrant Afro-fusion cultural scene, a rich sense of history and fine colonial architecture. Beyond it lie the Cape Peninsula, magnificent beaches and, of course, the lush Winelands to explore.

1 Company's Garden

This park was established by the first Dutch settlers in 1652 and features an eclectic mix of museums and galleries *(see pp12–13)*.

2 V&A Waterfront and Robben Island

Enjoy cafés, shops and bars at this waterfront complex. It is also the departure point for trips to Robben Island *(see pp14–17)*.

3 District Six Museum

This stirring Cape Town museum documents the apartheid-era evictions of "non-whites" from the central suburb of District Six to the remote Cape Flats *(see pp18–19)*.

4 Castle of Good Hope

Constructed in the 1660s and 1670s, South Africa's oldest extant building houses two museums. The ramparts overlook the Grand Parade, where crowds gathered to greet Nelson Mandela on his release from jail in 1990 *(see pp20–21)*.

5 Table Mountain

The thrilling aerial ascent of magnificent Table Mountain leads to a succession of stunning views over the Cape Peninsula and the Winelands *(see pp22–3)*.

6 Kirstenbosch National Botanical Garden

At its best during the spring wild-flower season, this garden preserves and propagates rare indigenous plant species and is a year-round visitor attraction (see pp26–7).

Groot Constantia Wine Estate 7

South Africa's oldest estate, Groot Constantia is noted for its old-world Cape Dutch architecture nestled amongst leafy vineyards (see pp28–9).

8 Simon's Town and Boulders Beach

With an abundance of quaint Victorian façades overlooking the splendid False Bay, this sleepy naval town is famed for the colony of adorable African penguins that waddles around on nearby Boulders Beach (see pp30–31).

Cape of Good Hope 9

Pink-hued proteas, grazing antelope and mischievous baboons can be observed at the peninsula's southern tip, where a clifftop lighthouse offers splendid bird's-eye views over Cape Point (see pp32–3).

Stellenbosch 10

Despite its wealth of impressive Cape Dutch architecture, South Africa's second-oldest town is better known – and justifiably so – as the most central base for exploring the renowned Winelands (see pp34–5).

🔟 ⭐ Company's Garden

This peaceful oasis at the heart of Cape Town, with stunning views of Table Mountain, is set amid the city's most important concentration of old buildings and museums. It was established by Jan van Riebeeck *(see p40)* in 1652 to provide fresh produce to passing Dutch ships. By the 18th century, it had been transformed into a world-renowned botanical garden and exported bulbs and other produce to Europe.

1 Parliament Buildings and Tuynhuys

On the southeast side are the Neo-Classical parliament buildings and the Tuynhuys **(above)**, the president's official Cape Town residence.

2 Rose Garden

The site of the Cape's first wine-producing vine and a source of rose-water in the Dutch era, this garden **(below)** contains many rose varieties, set out in a radial pattern.

Company's Garden

3 The Company's Garden Restaurant

With tables outside, as well as a choice of nest-like treehouses and swinging chairs, the restaurant is perfect for a light lunch or a good cup of coffee.

④ Aviary and Slave Bell

The aviary opposite The Company's Garden Restaurant houses many indigenous birds. The so-called Slave Bell is actually a fire bell from Greenmarket Square.

⑤ VOC Vegetable Garden

Inspired by the layout of the historical vegetable garden, this tribute to the park's original purpose highlights the need for urban food gardens.

⑥ Iziko Slave Lodge

Founded in 1679, this handsome building, once an unsanitary and cramped slaves' home, is now a museum charting the history of the slave trade.

⑦ Iziko South African Museum and Planetarium

This fine 19th-century mansion displays natural history, rock art and artifacts. Beside it stands the planetarium.

⑧ St George's Cathedral

This Anglican cathedral **(right)** was a centre of political protest during the 1980s. The oldest part of the building is a crypt designed by Sir Herbert Baker.

⑨ Iziko South African National Gallery

From an initial bequest of 45 paintings in 1871, the gallery is now the sub-Saharan region's leading art museum. Along with African and European collections, it has temporary shows.

ARCHBISHOP DESMOND TUTU

Desmond Tutu (b.1931), the first black Archbishop of Cape Town, was the bishop of St George's Cathedral. During his tenure, the church was a key centre of the anti-apartheid movement. Post-apartheid, this 1984 Nobel Peace Prize winner chaired the Truth and Reconciliation Commission (1995–2002).

⑩ Delville Wood Memorial

With sculptures by Anton van Wouw and Alfred Turner, this memorial **(below)** was unveiled in 1930 to commemorate the many South African casualties of World War I at Delville Wood, France.

NEED TO KNOW

MAP P5 ■ Entrances on Queen Victoria St and Adderley St ■ www.iziko.org.za

The Company's Garden Restaurant: 021 423 2919. Open 7am–6pm daily. www.thecompanys garden.com

Iziko South African Museum and Planetarium: Open 10am–5pm daily.

Museum: adm R30 (adults), R15 (kids 6–18 yrs), under 5s free. Planetarium: adm R40 (adults), R20 (kids under 19)

Iziko Slave Lodge: Open 10am–5pm Mon–Sat. Adm R30 (adults), R15 (kids 6–18 yrs), under 5s free

Iziko South African National Gallery: Open 10am–5pm daily. Adm R30 (adults), R15 (kids 6–18 yrs), under 5s free

TOP 10 ★ V&A Waterfront

Set between the sparkling waters of the Atlantic and majestic Table Mountain, the V&A Waterfront is integral to modern-day Cape Town, and reconnects the city to the sea. The complex opened in 1992 and has played a key role in reversing the economic decline that had gripped the old docklands since the 1960s. A working harbour to this day, the V&A Waterfront is South Africa's most-visited tourist destination, with a huge choice of eateries, shops, sights and leisure activities, including tours to Robben Island.

1 Two Oceans Aquarium
Highlights here **(above)** include Rockhopper and African penguins, the kelp forest and the predator exhibit. Try to visit at feeding times.

2 Cape Wheel
An iconic landmark, this 40-m (130-ft) observation wheel **(right)** has 30 air-conditioned cabins and offers a four-revolution ride lasting between 12 to 15 minutes.

HISTORY OF THE DOCKLANDS

The docklands started to take shape in the 19th century, when Prince Alfred (son of Queen Victoria) began the construction of the Alfred Basin by tipping a load of stones into the sea in 1860. Despite extensive development over the years, several Victorian buildings at the waterfront, such as the Ferryman and Mitchell's Pubs and Breakwater Lodge, are still standing.

3 Alfred Mall
Lined with alfresco bars and cafés, this converted Edwardian warehouse is an excellent spot to down refreshments while soaking up the idyllic views over the harbour to Table Mountain.

4 Harbour and Bay Cruises
You can take harbour tours, seal-watching trips and sunset cruises in Table Bay with one of the boat operators found on Quay 5.

5 Swing Bridge and Clock Tower
A piece of ornate Victoriana, the iconic Clock Tower **(right)** dates back to 1882. It is reached via a modern swing bridge that opens to accommodate passing boats.

NEED TO KNOW

MAP P2, Q1–2 ■ Information Centre, Dock Rd ■ 021 408 7600 ■ www.waterfront.co.za

Shops: Open 9am–9pm daily.

Cape Wheel: 021 418 2502. Open 11am–10pm Thu–Tue. Adm R100 (adults), R50 (kids 4–15 yrs). www.capewheel.co.za

Two Oceans Aquarium: Dock Rd; 021 418 3823. Open 9:30am–6pm daily. Adm R150 (adults). www.aquarium.co.za

Chavonnes Battery Museum: Clock Tower Precinct; 021 416 6230. Open 9am–4pm daily. Adm R70 (adults), R30 (kids 6–16 yrs). www.chavonnesbattery.co.za

■ There are many bars, restaurants and cafés to choose from (see p76).

V&A Waterfront

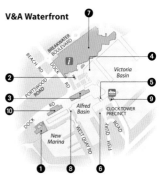

⑥ Chavonnes Battery Museum

This 18th-century fort was partially demolished to build the breakwater in 1861. What remains today offers an interesting look at the early maritime history of Cape Town.

⑦ Victoria Wharf Shopping Mall

Shop till you drop or dine at one of the many restaurants, then catch a movie at the Art Nouveau or Nu Metro cinemas – all in one of South Africa's largest malls.

⑧ Nobel Square

Life-sized statues of four Nobel Peace Prize winners – Albert Luthuli, Desmond Tutu, F W de Klerk and Nelson Mandela – are set alongside Noria Mabasa's intriguing Makonde-style sculpture.

⑨ Nelson Mandela Gateway

This is the embarkation point for day tours to Robben Island. It also displays photographs and information documenting the island's history.

⑩ The Watershed

Over 150 stalls in South Africa's largest indoor craft market (above) offer everything from African beadwork to tarot readings and holistic health treatments.

TOP 10 ⭐ Robben Island

Robben Island, in Table Bay, is South Africa's version of Alcatraz and has been a place of exile since Van Riebeeck's day. Its first political prisoner, a rebellious local trader named Autshumatom, was sent here in 1658. By the 1760s, the island held 70 prisoners. It is best known for its role under apartheid, when Nelson Mandela, Walter Sisulu, Govan Mbeki (father of Thabo Mbeki) and Jacob Zuma among others were held here. The last prisoner left in 1996, and the island is now a museum.

Maximum Security Block ①

With tours conducted by former political prisoners, this block **(right)** is the sombre highlight of a visit to Robben Island. Tours include a peek into Mandela's tiny cell and a look at photos of that era.

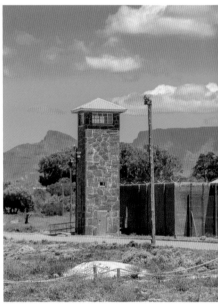

② Murray's Bay Harbour

Robben Island's small harbour is host to a large breeding colony of African penguins **(above)**. The island hosts about 132 bird species, including a large number of African black oystercatchers.

③ Jan van Riebeeck Quarry

The blue slate used as paving in the building of the Castle of Good Hope was quarried by Van Riebeeck at the far south of the island. The quarry closed in 1963.

④ Robben Island Village

Formerly home to prison wardens, this village comprises residential quarters for the museum staff. It also has two old churches, the Church of the Good Shepherd, built in 1895, and the Garrison Church, dating back to 1841.

⑤ Leper's Graveyard

This cemetery **(left)**, seen from the bus tour, is testament to the island's role as a leper colony from 1846 to 1930.

6 Lighthouse

Not open to visitors, the lighthouse **(left)** was built in 1864 on Minto Hill, the island's highest point. It replaced the fire beacons that were once in use.

7 Ferry Trip

The 30-minute ferry trip from the V&A Waterfront is best on calm, clear days, which provide fabulous views across Table Bay. Keep a look out for dolphins and seals.

8 Kramat of Tuan Guru

The island tour includes a stop at the shrine of Tuan Guru, an Indonesian Islamic cleric who was jailed here by the Dutch in the 18th century.

9 Robert Sobukwe Complex

A depressing sight, this is where anti-apartheid activist Robert Sobukwe was held in solitary confinement in 1963–9.

10 Limestone Quarry

Mandela and other prisoners undertook hard labour here. In 1990, former prisoners built a cairn **(right)**.

NELSON MANDELA

Mandela, born in 1918, was the first member of his family to attend school. His political career began in 1944, when, along with Oliver Tambo and Walter Sisulu, he formed the African National Congress Youth League. Mandela was accused of high treason in 1956, but the charges were dropped after a four-year trial. However, he was captured and incarcerated on Robben Island in 1964 under charges of treason. Released from jail in 1990, he went on to win the Nobel Peace Prize in 1993 and became president of South Africa in 1994. He stepped down in 1999, and died in 2013.

Robben Island

NEED TO KNOW

MAP A2 ■ Departures from the Nelson Mandela Gateway at the waterfront ■ 021 413 4200 ■ www. robben-island.org.za

Boats at 9am, 11am, 1pm, (Apr–Sep: also 3pm) weather permitting; guided tours with return ferry ride: 3½–4 hours.

Adm R320 (adults), R180 (kids under 18)

■ Book in advance online and arrive 30 minutes prior to the scheduled departure time of the boat.

■ There are no dining facilities on the island, but refreshments are for sale at the small curio shop.

TOP10 ⭐ District Six Museum

Founded in 1994, this award-winning community museum draws on a rich repository of artifacts and recollections supplied by the forcibly dispossessed residents of District Six. They celebrate everyday life as it was in a once-vibrant multicultural suburb that was re-zoned as a whites-only area under the Group Areas Act during the apartheid era *(see p40)*. Possibly the most moving of Cape Town's many museums, it provides some insight into the insidious effects of the racial discrimination propagated by the government on ordinary people.

① Little Wonder Store

It might be small, but this bookshop **(above)** on the ground floor stocks a comprehensive selection of titles about District Six and the many other mass evictions undertaken by the apartheid regime.

② Methodist Church

The Buitenkant Methodist Church, left standing after most of District Six was razed to the ground in 1966, became a place of contemplation for former residents and was chosen as the site for the museum in 1994.

③ Barbershop Display

This cheerfully nostalgic exhibit is a reconstruction of a typical 1950s' District Six barbershop, complete with period advertising plates pinned to the wall.

④ Nomvuyo's Room

This exhibit **(right)** re-creates the single room that was home to the author Nomvuyo Ngcelwane, her parents and three siblings before their eviction.

⑤ Bloemhof Flats Display

These poignant displays show photographs of Bloemhof Flats, a multiple-block housing development that was built over slummy Wells Square and famed for its football team.

THE DESTRUCTION OF DISTRICT SIX

Cape Town's sixth municipal district was established in 1867 on the slopes below Devil's Peak. Its residents were freed slaves, immigrants, and people of mixed race. The forced removal of black residents by the police began in 1901; by 1967, 60,000 residents had been removed to the Cape Flats. The first to return post-apartheid were handed their house keys by Mandela.

"Formation, Resistance, Restitution" Wall Panels ⑥

Using a combination of pictures, hard facts and interviews with former residents, this series of three wall panels **(right)** recounts the history of District Six since its creation in 1867.

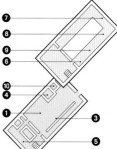

District Six Museum

Key to Floorplan
- Ground floor
- First floor

⑧ Sound Domes

Place your shoes on the marked footprint in front of the mural on the inside front wall of the first floor, and listen to a sequence of ten different stories narrated by former residents of District Six.

⑨ Tribute to Langarm Pioneers

Grainy photographs, period recordings and a stack of 78s rpm discs by swing musicians form a tantalizing introduction to the distinctively South African Langarm "jazz" music that rocked District Six during the 1930s, 1940s and 1950s.

⑦ Painted Floor Map

In the main hall **(above)**, a hand-painted street map of District Six before its demise is annotated by former residents with the locations of their houses before the bulldozers arrived.

⑩ The Story of Horstley Street

The memorial hall charts the history of Horstley Street. The mosaic and concrete floor includes extracts from written recollections of its residents.

NEED TO KNOW

MAP Q5 ▪ 25A Buitenkant St ▪ 021 466 7200
▪ www.districtsix.co.za

Open 9am–4pm Mon–Sat, Sun by appt

Adm R30 (self-guided tours), R45 (hourly guided tours), R15 (kids under 16)

▪ Many guided township tours start with a peek into District Six Museum, but it is also worth visiting independently to absorb the poignant exhibits.

▪ The District Six Museum Café serves coffee, light snacks, local sweets, such as *koeksisters,* and Cape Malay-inspired lunches, including *bobotie,* tomato *bredie* and spicy chicken curry.

TOP 10 ⭐ Castle of Good Hope

Constructed between 1666 and 1679, the imposing Castle of Good Hope is the oldest functional building in South Africa. It was built with slate quarried on Robben Island and sandstone from Lion's Head, a small mountain between Table Mountain and Signal Hill. Originally located alongside Table Bay to protect the new Dutch settlement from naval invasion, its seaward wall now stands about 1 km (half a mile) inland after land reclamation. Following an extensive program of restoration that took place during 1969–93, it now houses two permanent museums and hosts occasional temporary exhibitions.

1 Governor's and Secunde Houses

Part of the 12-m- (39-ft-) high inner wall that bisects the courtyard, the Governor's and Secunde's houses were built by Simon van der Stel in the 1690s to accommodate himself and his *secunde* (second-in-command).

2 Main Entrance

Built in 1683 the main entrance is notable for its bell tower **(below)** made of imported yellow *ystelsteen* and sculpted masonry depicting a lion with seven arrows to represent the provinces of The Netherlands. The key ceremony, which symbolizes the ceremonial unlocking of the castle, is held here on weekdays.

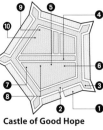

3 Kat Balcony

This elegant and ornate balcony **(above)** has an Anton Anreith bas-relief sculpture. During Dutch colonial times, it was the ceremonial site for greeting visitors and for the reading out of judicial sentences.

Castle of Good Hope

4 William Fehr Collection

This collection, donated by Dr William Fehr, includes paintings by Thomas Baines. Other works give insight into the lives of early settlers.

5 "Fired" Ceramics

This exhibition **(left)** features a rare collection of African pottery, with one of the renowned "Lydenburg Heads" dating to around AD 500.

6 Inner Archway and Old Well

The inner archway is flanked by the covered well that once provided water to castle residents, and has a memorial to the dead of World War I.

7 Block B

The castle's oldest section, to the right of the main entrance, dates from the 1660s. A staircase leads to the grassy bastion, offering fine views out across the Grand Parade.

8 Dungeon and Torture Chamber

This room was the site where prisoners were tortured, in accordance with the Dutch law that required a confession before sentencing.

CITY HALL

Cape Town had no city hall prior to 1905, when the foundation was laid in front of the Grand Parade opposite the castle. The Italian Renaissance-style building houses an opulent interior with marble staircases and a stained-glass window commemorating King Edward VII. On his release from jail, Mandela made his first public speech from its balcony.

9 Military Museum

The Cape's military past, from the first clash between Bartolomeu Dias *(see p40)* and the locals in 1488 to the 1899–1902 South African War, is documented here **(left)**.

10 Leeuhek and Moat

Visitors can gain entrance to the castle by crossing its moat **(above)**. On the way is the Leeuhek (Lion's Gate), a sentry portal, which was built in 1720 and is crowned with two lion sculptures.

NEED TO KNOW

MAP Q5 ■ Corner of Strand & Darling sts ■ 021 787 1260 ■ www. castleofgoodhope.co.za

Open 9am–4pm daily; free guided tours at 11am, noon, 2pm daily

Adm R30 (adults), R15 (kids 5–18 yrs), under 4s free

■ If you visit on a weekday, aim to be at the main gate at 10am or noon, first for the key ceremony and then for the firing of the signal cannon.

■ Situated inside the castle to the left of the main entrance gate, De Goewerneur Restaurant (021 787 1202; open 9am–4pm daily) serves inexpensive snacks and light meals that have a Cape Malay influence. There is outdoor seating under the colonnades.

🔟 ⭐ Table Mountain

South Africa's most celebrated geographical landmark, Table Mountain dominates the Cape Town skyline from almost every direction. This remarkably flat (hence the name) sandstone plateau is sometimes swathed in the cloudy shroud that locals refer to as the "tablecloth". Most people reach the top using the cableway that opened in 1929 and has since taken over 25 million passengers to the summit. The main attraction of the summit is the fabulous views, which capture Cape Town and the Peninsula in their full glory.

2 Abseil Africa
A must for the adventurous traveller is Abseil Africa's 112-m (367-ft) abseil route down the ledge of Table Mountain overlooking Camps Bay (see p53).

3 Platteklip Gorge Trail
This demanding but popular alternative to the cableway runs from Maclear's Beacon to Tafelberg Road.

4 Dassies and Other Animals
Look for the rock hyrax, or dassie, a guinea pig lookalike often seen basking on the rocky plateau. Other wildlife includes klipspringer and gaudy agama lizards.

1 Cableway
Travel in a small circular cable car (above), complete with rotating floor and 360° views of Cape Town and Table Bay. The incredible 5-minute ride to the top seems too short, and comes within inches of the sheer cliff face below the Upper Cableway Station.

TIPS FOR WALKERS

Table Mountain has several well-marked trails to the summit, and these are graded according to difficulty. Hikers must wear proper walking boots and are advised to check with the Lower Cableway Station before setting out, as weather conditions may change without warning. Hiking on windy or misty days is not recommended.

5 Upper Cableway Viewpoint
Emerge from the Upper Cableway Station for a view of Signal Hill, Robben Island in Table Bay and the Hottentots Holland on the eastern horizon.

Table Mountain viewed from Robben Island

6 Fynbos Vegetation

A sweeping glance over Table Mountain's sandstone plateau might be your first exposure to *fynbos*, a heath-like cover **(above)** with muted shades offset by fiery pink proteas, multicoloured disas and spectral silver trees.

8 Maclear's Beacon

The highest point on Table Mountain **(left)** is marked by an 1865 cairn. It is an attractive goal for peak-baggers and ramblers, and there's some great scenery along the way, too.

7 Dassie, Agama and Klipspringer Trails

These three circular, paved paths, although not teeming with wildlife, offer glorious views and are wheelchair friendly. Dassie is the shortest.

9 Birdlife

The *fynbos* attracts nectar-dependent sun-birds and sugarbirds. The redwing starling and chat often visit the summit. Look out for swifts, kestrels and black eagles.

10 Sign 15 Viewpoint

This viewpoint offers sweeping vistas over the mountainous spine of the Cape Peninsula, with glimpses of Simon's Town and Kommetjie through the hills.

NEED TO KNOW

MAP H1 ■ Tafelberg Rd ■ 021 424 8181 ■ www.tablemountain.net

Cable cars leave every 10–15 minutes from 8:30am–4:30pm in mid-winter and 8am–8:30pm in midsummer. Free, guided 30-min walks hourly, 9am–3pm daily

Fare R135 one-way or R255 return (adults), R65 one-way or R125 return (kids 4–17 yrs)

- ■ **Book tickets online to avoid the queues.**

- ■ **The cableway is inoperable on days when mist and cloud settles on the mountain, so try to visit when the weather is good.**

- ■ **The Table Mountain Café with its breakfast buffet and gourmet deli, caters for all tastes.**

Kirstenbosch National Botanical Garden

One of the world's great botanical gardens, Kirstenbosch was established in 1913 to protect the immense floral wealth of the Western Cape. Set on the eastern slopes of Table Mountain, the lower sections of the garden are planted with lush indigenous flora, blending into a natural cover of *fynbos* and forest at higher altitudes, accessible by a network of footpaths.

Sunbird on a protea plant

1 Fynbos Walk

This footpath passes through colourful *fynbos* vegetation **(right)** unique to the Cape. The colourful proteas found here bloom in winter and spring, when they attract the long-tailed Cape sugarbird.

2 Visitors' Centre and Shop

At the entrance gate, the centre sells a good map of the garden. A gift shop **(above)** and bookshop, stocked with books about South Africa's flora and fauna, are also here.

3 Mathews Rockery

A labyrinthine collection of dry-country plants, including some massive euphorbia trees, this is most stunning in winter, when aloe blooms attract nectar-feeding sunbirds.

4 Tree Canopy Walkway

Opened to mark the garden's centenary, this walkway snakes along among the tree tops of the arboretum, giving magnificent views of Table Mountain.

5 Conservatory

The glass-topped conservatory **(left)** boasts several plants from arid southern African habitats. At the centre, a spectacular baobab, typical of the arid Kalahari, rises above other species.

Previous pages Delville Wood Memorial in the Company's Garden

Sculpture Garden ⑥

Situated in the eastern corner of Kirstenbosch, the sprawling Sculpture Garden is scattered with superb examples of contemporary stone sculptures **(right)**, created by artists in Zimbabwe's Shona tradition. Some are available for purchase.

⑧ Van Riebeeck's Hedge

This thick hedge of native wild almonds, planted by Jan van Riebeeck in 1660, marked the boundary of the new Cape Colony. The almond-like fruit of this plant is poisonous.

⑨ Useful Plants Garden

Complete with well-marked signs, this garden **(below)** has a selection of medical plants used to treat everything from headaches to secondary symptoms of HIV/AIDS.

⑦ Cycad Garden and the Dell

This section of the garden has large trees, a stream and a pool set below a natural amphitheatre with cycads that evolved 150–200 million years ago.

WILDLIFE IN THE GARDENS

Though best known for its plants, Kirstenbosch also supports varied fauna, and is home to 200 vertebrate species. The birds include the Cape sugarbird, the lesser double-collared sunbird, the spectacular black eagle that breeds on Table Mountain cliffs and the francolins that haunt the streams. Mammals include rock hyraxes and mongooses and two frog species that are found only on Table Mountain.

⑩ Vlei

A wooden boardwalk crosses the small reed-lined *vlei* (marsh), which is a magnet for a wide variety of birds as well as other wildlife, such as the rooikat, grysbok and mongoose, all of which are often spotted here.

NEED TO KNOW

MAP H2 ■ Rhodes Drive, Newlands ■ 021 799 8783 ■ www.sanbi.org/gardens/kirstenbosch

Open Apr–Aug: 8am–6pm daily; Sep–Mar: 8am–7pm daily

Adm R60 (adults), R15 (kids 6–17 yrs), under 6s free

Conservatory: **Open** 9am–5pm

■ Botany enthusiasts should time their visit to coincide with one of the free guided walks (Mon–Sat; see website for times).

■ **Sunday Summer Sunset Concerts are held from November to April** *(see p63).*

■ Moyo restaurant (021 762 9585) serves African specialities, and the Kirstenbosch Tea Room (021 797 4883) offers lighter snacks.

TOP 10 ⭐ Groot Constantia Wine Estate

Founded in 1685 by Simon van der Stel, Groot Constantia is the oldest wine-producing farm in South Africa. It boasts a wonderful setting below the Constantiaberg on the Cape Peninsula, and is situated about 10 km (6 miles) south of central Cape Town. Home to some of the country's most interesting Cape Dutch architecture, it features two gabled buildings completed under the late-18th-century proprietorship of Hendrik Cloete. It was under the Cloete family, who owned the farm from 1778 to 1885, that Constantia's dessert wines won international acclaim, and the estate became the official supplier to Napoleon Bonaparte, exiled on St Helena. Bought by the Cape Government in 1885, it has been a non-profit company since 1993.

3 Historic Gardens

Dotted with trees, some of which were planted in van der Stel's day, the estate gardens (right) are delightfully peaceful and make the ideal spot for a leisurely stroll. They afford lovely views of the vineyards and the sandstone Constantiaberg mountain range.

1 Jonkershuis

Expanded from an outbuilding, the thatched Jonkershuis (meaning the house of the eldest son or *jonkheer*) is an attractive Cape Dutch building with a fine restaurant (above).

2 Orientation Centre

The orientation centre is a useful first port of call, with its scale model of the estate and informative panels discussing the long history of the Constantia Estate.

4 Coach House Museum

The Isaacs Transport Collection is displayed in a courtyard behind the Jonkershuis. Exhibits include old coaches, carts, bicycles, and vintage mule and ox wagons.

NEED TO KNOW

MAP H2 ▪ Groot Constantia Rd ▪ 021 794 5128 ▪ www.groot constantia.co.za

Open 9am–6pm; hourly cellar tours 10am–4pm

Wine tasting: adm R75. Cellar tours: adm R100 (tasting included)

Homestead Museum: 021 795 5140. Open 10am–5pm daily. Adm R30 (adults). www.iziko.org.za

▪ The estate's restaurants stay open for dinner.

▪ Most visitors dash in and out to see the museums and sample the wines, but it's worth exploring this estate at leisure on foot.

7 Cloete Cellar

A long, narrow structure dating from 1791 **(left)**, the building has South Africa's famous triangular gable and a striking Rococo pediment sculpted by Anton Anreith. Originally used as a wine cellar, it now houses displays of antique wine storage and drinking vessels.

SIMON VAN DER STEL

One of the most influential figures of the early colonial era, Simon van der Stel was born at sea in 1639, son of Commander Adriaan van der Stel. He became commander of the Cape in 1679 and was upgraded to Governor in 1691. Van der Stel played a key role in the foundation of Stellenbosch and Simon's Town, both named after him. He retired in 1699 and dedicated himself to the development of Constantia, where he died peacefully in 1712.

8 Historic Gates and Main Drive

The magnificent main drive leads right up to the main complex, passing through a gate **(above)** that dates from the 18th century.

10 Wine-Tasting Cellar

Just inside the entrance gate, the wine-tasting and sales centre offers excellent wines for visitors to sample and buy. One of them, the highly praised Grand Constance, revives the historic dessert wine tradition that earned the estate its fame.

5 Historic Bath

This ornate oval pool, located on the Constantiaberg slopes, is of uncertain origin, but it is similar in style to the gable of the main house, which dates from the late 18th century.

6 Manor House Façade

Expanding on van der Stel's house, Hendrik Cloete later added the front gables and commissioned the sculpture by Anton Anreith in the niche.

9 Homestead Museum

This museum in the manor house is decorated in a style typical of an 18th-century estate owner **(above)**. The old Cape furniture and art were donated by collector Alfred de Pass in 1927.

TOP 10 ⭐ Simon's Town and Boulders Beach

Simon's Town is named after the first Cape Colony Governor Simon van der Stel, who selected its harbour as a safe winter alternative to Table Bay. With a 144-year tenure as Britain's main regional naval base, prior to the South African navy taking over in 1957, it is lent a distinct character by its wealth of Victorian architecture and lovely location on steep slopes above a string of sandy beaches. Most famous of these is Boulders Beach, with its African penguins.

1 Boulders Beach
The sheltering rocks after which Boulders (above) is named make it a lovely, secluded spot for a swim, and, if you're lucky, you might find yourself taking a paddle with a penguin *(see p46)*.

2 South African Naval Museum
Set in a masthouse and sail loft from the 1740s, this museum features a life-size replica ship's bridge, complete with simulated rocking motion.

3 Jubilee Square and Quay
Overlooking the harbour are Jubilee Square and Quayside Mall (below). Boat trips launch from the jetty to explore False Bay and Seal Island.

4 Historic Mile
The concentration of venerable buildings in Simon's Town is at its most dense along the so-called Historic Mile – a succession of Victorian façades that run down St George's Street (above). Stop by the bar at the Lord Nelson Hotel, built in 1929.

5 Willis Walk

Situated outside the national park, this wheelchair-friendly boardwalk **(left)** offers opportunities to spot penguins and their offspring, and *fynbos* birds such as Cape canaries and martins.

6 Foxy Beach

You'll see several hundred penguins here surfing or strutting on the sandy beach. Before heading along the boardwalks to view the birds, brush up your penguin knowledge at the handy Boulders Visitor Centre.

7 Seaforth Beach

Sheltered by rocks and occasionally visited by penguins from nearby Boulders, Seaforth offers safe swimming in calm weather. Its popular beachfront restaurant is a welcome retreat when the wind gets too strong.

BOULDERS BEACH ORIENTATION

Boulders lies to the south of Simon's Town and is accessed from the main road to Cape Point. Foxy and Boulders Beaches lie within an annexe of Table Mountain National Park and are entered via two separate gates. The Boulders Visitor Centre is at the Foxy Beach gate. Willis Walk, which connects the two gates, is outside the park and is open at all times.

8 Metrorail Southern Line

The Metrorail service **(above)** that begins in Cape Town is one of the world's great suburban train rides, offering breathtaking views on its way to Simon's Town's Victorian railway station.

9 Kayaking

For an alternative view of the coast and its penguins, hire a kayak at Simon's Town harbour for a 2-hour guided paddling trip to Boulders Beach and back.

10 Simon's Town Museum

Built as a Governor's Residence, this museum houses an exhibition on apartheid's forced removals and a more lighthearted display about a naval dog.

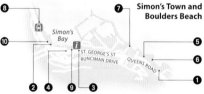

Simon's Town and Boulders Beach

Simon's Bay

ST. GEORGE'S ST
RUNCIMAN DRIVE QUEENS ROAD

NEED TO KNOW

MAP H4 ■ Simon's Town Visitor Centre ■ 111 St George's St ■ 021 786 8440 ■ www.simonstown.com

Boulders Visitor Centre/ Penguin Colonies: 021 786 2329; www.sanparks.org. Open Feb–Mar & Oct–Nov: 8am–6:30pm daily (Apr–Sep: to 5pm), Dec–Jan: 7am–7:30pm daily. Adm R70 (adults), R35 (kids)

Metrorail Southern Line: 080 065 6463; www. getgometro.com

Kayaking: Kayak Cape Town; 082 501 8930; www.kayakcapetown. co.za. Adm R300

Simon's Town Museum: Court Rd; 021 786 3046. Open 10am–4pm Mon–Fri, 10am–1pm Sat

■ Dine at the Seaforth Restaurant *(see p89)* or Bertha's in Quayside Mall.

TOP 10 ★ Cape of Good Hope

Though Cape Point is not the southernmost point in Africa, most visitors walk away with the distinct sensation that they've seen the end of the continent – such is the scenic drama of the storm-battered headland, whose precipitous cliffs rise to 250 m (820 ft) from the vast blue sea. The Cape of Good Hope (part of Table Mountain National Park) is also of interest for its wealth of fauna. It has a cover of pastel-hued *fynbos*, with more plant species than are indigenous to the entire British Isles.

1 Rooikrans

Just 1 km (half a mile) from the main road to Cape Point, this superb viewpoint **(above)** is the best spot for seasonal whale watching. A footpath leads to the rocky beach below.

2 Gifkommetjie Circular Drive

This road loop leads through subtly shaded fields of *fynbos* to a ridge studded with mushroom-like, balancing rock formations. The views are stunning, and energetic visitors can follow the little-used 3-hour walking trail to *Hoek van Bobbejaan* (Baboon's Corner). Look out for wild tortoises.

NEED TO KNOW
MAP H6

Table Mountain National Park: 021 780 9010; www. capepoint.co.za. Open Oct–Mar: 6am–6pm, Apr–Sep: 7am–5pm. Adm R135 (adults), R70 (kids 2–11 yrs)

Cape Point Ostrich Farm: 021 780 9294; www.cape pointostrichfarm.com.

Open 9:30am–5:30pm daily. Half-hourly tours R55 (adults), R25 (kids 6–16 yrs)

Funicular: return trip R65 (adults), R25 (kids 2–11 yrs)

■ Wild chacma baboons are common here. They can be aggressive if you are carrying food.

■ By the car park, the Two Oceans Restaurant serves meals during the day.

3 Cape Point Ostrich Farm

Near the park entrance, this private ostrich farm **(right)** lets you get close to the world's largest bird. They offer ostrich-derived souvenirs, and you can even sample a tasty ostrich platter.

6 Climb/Funicular to Cape Point

The final ascent to spectacular Cape Point involves either a steep footpath, or taking the funicular **(left)** – a rope-supported railway car designed to cope with such gradients.

7 Buffelsfontein Visitor Centre

This pretty Cape Dutch farmhouse should be your first stop if you plan to explore the area. Apart from a stock of books and leaflets about the reserve, it also houses a natural history museum.

FALSE BAY WHALES

Between July and November, the whales that pass through False Bay can be observed from Rooikrans and other beaches along the reserve's eastern seaboard. The most common is the southern right whale, which can easily reach a length of around 15 m (49 ft). It is also possible to glimpse Bryde's whales, humpback whales and killer whales (orcas). For news of recent sightings, call 079 391 2105 or visit www.awhaleofa heritageroute.co.za.

4 Buffels Bay

This sandy, surf-washed arc is a great place for a picnic lunch – there are even *braai* (barbecue) facilities available, though keep an eye out for baboons. There's also a tidal pool for safe swimming.

8 Bordjiesdrif

The tidal pools are good for marine life, and the artificial rock pool above the beach is safe to swim in. Sights here include a cross in honour of Vasco da Gama's landing in 1497, and the igneous Black Rock.

10 Cape of Good Hope Footpath

The 90-minute return trail **(above)**, from the car park to the Cape of Good Hope beach below, offers magnificent views of the lighthouse and plenty of opportunities for good marine bird-watching.

5 Kanonkop Walk

A short walking trail that starts at Buffelsfontein, Kanonkop Walk leads to the old signal cannon after which it is named. It passes a 19th-century lime kiln and offers some splendid views across False Bay. Look out for the blue disa that flowers here in January and February.

Cape Point Lighthouse 9

Built from 1913 to 1919 using rocks carried by hand from the present-day car park, this is South Africa's brightest lighthouse **(right)**. It stands at 238 m (781 ft) above sea level on the highest section of Cape Point's rocky peak.

TOP 10 ⭐ Stellenbosch

Founded by Simon van der Stel in 1679, Stellenbosch is the second-oldest town in South Africa, and arguably the most beautiful of all. Running northwards from the banks of the Eerste River below the Jonkershoek Mountains, the stately avenues of this university town are lined with venerable Cape Dutch buildings and the shady trees that earned it the nickname of Eikestad (Town of Oaks). This old-world ambience is offset by a contemporary array of restaurants, cafés, bars and shops. The short drive to nearby Franschhoek via the Helshoogte Pass is packed with must-see sights *(see pp36–7)*.

Dorp Streetl ④
The best-preserved road in Stellenbosch, Dorp Street is lined with pre-20th-century Cape Dutch buildings. The finest façades **(right)** are between the junctions of Herte and Drostdy streets.

① Botanical Garden
The petite but leafy Botanical Garden **(above)**, the town's best-kept secret, is particularly notable for its collections of *fynbos* plants, ferns, orchids and bonsai tress, and for its dry-country succulents from Namibia.

⑤ Lanzerac Wine Estate
This is the closest wine estate to Stellenbosch. First planted with vines in 1692, it was then known as Schoongezicht (Beautiful View). Its excellent wines and a fine restaurant make it worth a detour.

② Die Bergkelder Wine Centre
This distinctive building, found nestled below the Papegaaiberg, has more than 200 wines. Taste the Cape's finest produce in the atmospheric cellar.

Village Museum ③
Each of this museum's four charming period-furnished houses **(right)** represents phases in the town's development; the most recent one dates from the 1830s.

MERRIMAN
DU TOIT
BIRD
RYNEVELD
VICTORIA
(1 mile)
ALEXANDER
VAN RIEBEECK
ADAM TAS
STRAND
MARKET
PIET RETIEF
DORP
Eerste

Stellenbosch

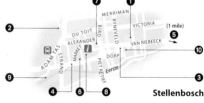

Oom Samie Se Winkel 6
Named after former owner Oom (Uncle) Samie Volsteedt, this landmark trading post (see p94) stocks homemade sweets, traditional handicrafts and Africana **(right)**.

The Braak 7
The village green (braak) is enclosed by historic buildings, notably the Anglican, thatch-roofed Church of St Mary (1852) with its combined Neo-Gothic and Cape Dutch influences, and the Rhenish Church (1823), with a Baroque pulpit.

Toy and Miniature Museum 8
Housed in a Rhenish parsonage, this museum has tiny houses, antique dolls and other nostagic toys, plus a perfectly re-created Blue Train, which travels from a miniature Stellenbosch to Matjiesfontein.

UNIVERSITY OF STELLENBOSCH
South Africa's premier Afrikaans university started life in 1866 as the Stellenbosch Gymnasium, set in a building that still stands on Dorp Street. The university alumni include four of South Africa's prime ministers (Jan Smuts, D F Malan, J B M Hertzog and H F Verwoerd) and anti-apartheid activists such as Beyers Naudé and Heinrich Grosskopf. The town's Botanical Garden was founded by the university in 1922.

Rupert Museum 9
To the town's southwest, this museum of South African art shows works by artists such as Irma Stern and Walter Battiss.

Moederkerk 10
Opposite the Village Museum, on the site of the original Dutch Reformed Church that burned down in 1710, is the Moederkerk (Mother Church), a tall Neo-Gothic building with a steeple that was completed in 1866.

NEED TO KNOW

MAP D2 ■ Tourist Office ■ 36 Market St ■ 021 883 3584

Toy and Miniature Museum: Market St; 021 882 8861. Open from 9am Mon–Sat. Adm R15 (adults), R5 (kids 3–18 yrs)

Rupert Museum: Stellentia Ave; 021 888 3344. Open 10am–4pm Mon–Sat. Adm R20 (adults), R10 (kids)

Village Museum: 37 Ryneveld St; 021 887 2948. Open daily. Adm R30 (adults), R5 (kids)

Botanical Garden: Cnr Neethling & Van Riebeeck sts. Open daily

Die Bergkelder Wine Centre: George Blake St; 021 809 8025. Open from 9am Mon–Sat. Adm R60

Lanzerac Wine Estate: 1 Lanzerac Rd; 021 887 1132. Tasting daily. Adm R65

■ For details of restaurants in Stellenbosch, see p98.

Stellenbosch to Franschhoek

Boschendal wine estate, between the Drakenstein and Simonsberg ranges

1 Boschendal
MAP E2 ■ Pniel Rd, Groot Drakenstein ■ 021 870 4210/11 (tasting); 021 870 4274 (picnic reservation) ■ Tasting 10am–5pm Mon–Thu, 10am–6pm Fri–Sun; cellar tours: 10:30am, noon, 1:30pm & 3pm daily; tasting fee ■ www.boschendal.com

At the gateway to the Franschhoek Valley, Boschendal offers wine-tasting and picnic baskets for a decadent lunch.

2 Pniel
MAP E2

Founded by the Berlin Mission Society in 1834 to house former slaves,

pretty Pniel, below the Simonsberg, remained zoned for black people during apartheid, despite its location. A 19th-century church and the 1992 Freedom Monument marking the emancipation of slaves are landmarks.

3 Franschhoek Motor Museum
MAP F2 ■ R45 towards Franschhoek ■ 021 874 9000 ■ Open 10am–4pm Mon–Fri, 10am–3pm Sat–Sun ■ Adm ■ www.fmm.co.za

Motor Museum racing car

In the prestigious L'Ormarins Estate, this museum is a magnet for car enthusiasts. The collection of over 220 rare vehicles includes an 1898 Beeston motor tricycle and a 2003 Ferrari Enzo.

4 Delaire Graff and Tokara Wine Estates
Delaire Graff: MAP E2; Helshoogte Pass Rd; 021 885 8160; tasting 10am–5pm Mon–Sat, 10am–4pm Sun; tasting fee; www.delaire.co.za ■ Tokara: MAP E2; Helshoogte Rd; 021 808 5900; tasting 9am–5pm Mon–Fri, 10am–5pm Sat, Sun; tasting fee; www.tokara.co.za

These estates, perched on the rim of Helshoogte Pass, are best saved for the end of the day, when superb views over the Winelands can be enjoyed at sunset over a glass of the local bubbly.

THE HUGUENOTS

This group was formed of Protestants who fled France to escape Catholic persecution under Louis XIV. Franschhoek is a legacy to their influx to the Cape in 1688. Due partly to an edict that Dutch should be the sole language of education, local government and commerce, the Huguenots swiftly integrated into the established culture. They were major contributors to South Africa's emergence as a top wine producer. Many Afrikaans surnames are of French origin – some, such as De Villiers, have survived, while others have adapted, such as Cronjé (Cronier) and Nel (Neél).

5 Mont Rochelle
MAP F2 ■ Dassenberg Rd
■ 021 876 2770 ■ www.virginlimited
edition.com/en/mont-rochelle
■ Tasting 10am–7pm daily; tasting fee

A 5-minute drive – or a steep half-hour walk – from Franschhoek, this small wine estate boasts lovely thatched Cape Dutch buildings. It offers a great view over the Franschhoek Valley and Middagkrans Mountains, best enjoyed from the two fine restaurants here.

6 La Motte
There's plenty to see and do at this excellent estate. Join a tutored themed wine tasting, or simply sample their award-winning reds, whites and bubbly under your own steam. Take a guided walk around the extensive grounds, nose around the fascinating museum and then visit the Pierneef à La Motte restaurant for an exquisite lunch or afternoon tea (see p96).

La Motte's elegant restaurant

7 Huguenot Monument
MAP F2 ■ Lambrechts Rd
■ Open 9am–5pm daily ■ Adm

This stone monument, built on the outskirts of Franschhoek in 1938–48, commemorates the arrival of the

The Winelands

Symbolic Huguenot Monument

Huguenots in 1688. The three high arches represent the holy trinity, while a statue of a woman on a globe displays various religious symbols.

8 Hillcrest Berry Orchards
MAP E2 ■ 021 885 1629 ■ Helshoogte Pass Rd ■ Open 9am–5pm daily
■ www.hillcrestberries.co.za

Hillcrest, about 10 km (6 miles) from Stellenbosch, cultivates seven types of berries. Its confections can be tasted at the restaurant or bought at the gift shop.

9 Dutch Reformed Church
MAP F2 ■ Huguenot Rd

Franschhoek's architectural gem, the Dutch Reformed Church, was built in 1848. Set below the surrounding mountains, the church's whitewashed gables and 19th-century bell tower make a pretty, pastoral picture.

10 Huguenot Memorial Museum
MAP F2 ■ Lambrechts Rd ■ 021 876 2532 ■ Open 9am–5pm Mon–Sat, 2–5pm Sun ■ Adm ■ www.museum.co.za

This excellent museum documents the daily life of the French settlers who gave Franschhoek its name. There is a fine collection of old Bibles, including one printed in 1636.

The Top 10 of Everything

A colony of African penguins waddling
across the sands at Boulders Beach

⏏️🔟 Moments in History

1 Prehistory

The earliest signs of human habitation along Table Bay date back 1.4 million years and consist of Stone Age tools of the Acheulean culture. San hunter-gatherers arrived around 30,000 years ago and left a legacy of rock-art sites, notably in the Cederberg Mountains north of Cape Town. Khoikhoi pastoralists first arrived with their fat-tailed sheep around 2,000 years ago.

2 The Portuguese Arrive

In 1488, Portuguese navigator Bartolomeu Dias became the first European to round the Cape. This led to a succession of clashes with the Khoikhoi that culminated in Captain d'Almeida's death in Table Bay in 1510.

Statue of Bartolomeu Dias

3 Foundation of Cape Town

In 1652, Jan van Riebeeck, an employee of the Dutch East India Company (VOC), founded a victual station in Table Bay to provide fresh produce to passing VOC ships. Within a century, Cape Town was home to settlers from Europe, though slaves outnumbered free citizens.

4 British Occupation and the Great Trek

The governance of Cape Town by the British in 1795 led to the emancipation of slaves in 1834. This so angered slave-owning Boers (Dutch farmers) that in the Great Trek of 1836–43 over 12,000 moved north, where they founded Boer Republics, notably the Free State and Transvaal.

5 South African War and Unionization

The South African War of 1899–1902 was initiated by English imperialists to gain control of the Johannesburg goldfields. This bloody three-year engagement led to the formation of the Union of South Africa in 1910, which comprised the Cape, Natal, Transvaal and the Free State. Former Boer general Louis Botha became the first prime minister.

6 Foundation of Apartheid

After the National Party (NP) was voted in by the electorate in 1948, parliamentary acts formalized racial inequities into the ideological monolith apartheid ("separateness").

Painting of Jan van Riebeeck and VOC members at the Cape of Good Hope

7 Sharpeville Massacre and Rivonia Trial

Resistance to apartheid was galvanized by the police massacre of 69 civilians at a peaceful protest at Sharpeville in 1960. This led to the formation of Umkhonto we Sizwe – the armed wing of the banned African National Congress (ANC) – under Nelson Mandela, who was convicted of treason with other anti-apartheid leaders in the Rivonia Trial of 1962–3.

8 Foundation of the UDF

In 1983, more than 15,000 anti-apartheid activists congregated at Mitchells Plain to form the United Democratic Front (UDF), effectively the domestic representative of the ANC in apartheid's dying years.

Nelson Mandela's release

9 Release of Nelson Mandela

President F W de Klerk lifted the ban on the ANC in February 1990, and Mandela was released from prison after 27 years. He made his first public speech after his imprisonment outside Cape Town's City Hall *(see p21)*.

10 Democracy

In May 1994, the ANC swept to victory in South Africa's first fully democratic elections, after securing eight of the nine provinces, the exception being the Western Cape, the last stronghold of the NP. Mandela was inaugurated as president.

TOP 10 FAMOUS SOUTH AFRICANS

Archbishop Desmond Tutu

1 Jan van Riebeeck
The founder of Cape Town, Dutch colonizer van Riebeeck was commander of the Cape until 1662.

2 Simon van der Stel
Commander and Governor of the Cape (1679–99), Simon van der Stel was the founder of Stellenbosch developed the famous Constantia wineries.

3 Cecil John Rhodes
British mining magnate Rhodes founded the diamond company De Beers, and was prime minister of the Cape from 1890 to 1895.

4 Nelson Mandela
South Africa's most famous son was incarcerated in prisons around Cape Town for 27 years *(see p17)*.

5 Archbishop Desmond Tutu
This Nobel Peace Prize winner served as Anglican Archbishop of Cape Town between 1985 and 1995 *(see p13)*.

6 Breyten Breytenbach (b. 1939)
This Cape Town-educated poet and novelist, imprisoned for anti-apartheid activities, now resides in France.

7 J M Coetzee
Booker Prize winner and recipient of the 2003 Nobel Prize for Literature.

8 Steve Biko
The anti-apartheid activist and founder of the Black Consciousness Movement died in police custody in 1977, aged 30.

9 Brenda Fassie
The "Madonna of the Townships" was a popular recording artist prior to her drug-related death in 2004.

10 Jacques Kallis
Kallis is considered one of South Africa's greatest cricketers.

🔟 Local Culture

Apartheid exhibits in the District Six Museum

1 District Six Museum

This emotionally charged museum is a testament to the iniquitous Group Areas Act passed by the National Party in the 1950s and 1960s. The museum focuses on day-to-day life in District Six before apartheid's bulldozers rumbled in *(see pp18–19)*.

2 Langa
MAP H1

Founded in 1927, the oldest black township in Cape Town was an integral part of the resistance to apartheid for the resident Xhosa people. Walking tours of Langa include the Gugu S'Thebe Arts Theatre and the middle-class area known as "Beverley Hills".

Mosaic in the Langa township

3 Iziko Slave Lodge

This building opposite the Company's Garden was founded in 1679 as quarters for the immigrants – the force behind the Cape's agricultural economy – who were imported from Malaysia and Indian Ocean islands. Now a museum, it charts the history of the slave trade through a series of multimedia displays *(see p13)*.

4 Rock Art Gallery, Iziko South African Museum
MAP P5 ■ 25 Queen Victoria St ■ 021 481 3800 ■ Open 10am–5pm daily ■ Adm ■ www.iziko.org.za

South Africa is one of the world's most important repositories of rock art, with several sites dating back 10,000 years scattered through the country. This gallery has a superb display, including re-creations and an original panel relocated here.

5 Gugulethu
MAP H2

Join a tour or visit "Gugs" under your own steam (but never after dark). This up-and-coming township is home to Mzoli's, a *braai* (barbecue) restaurant, where you buy meat from the butcher then take it to be grilled.

6 Meet a Former Political Prisoner on Robben Island

A trip to Robben Island ends with a tour of the maximum-security prison where anti-apartheid activists were incarcerated (see pp16–17). Here a former political prisoner gives an account of the island's history, their activism and time in prison.

7 Khayelitsha
MAP C3

An isiXhosa phrase meaning "Our New Home", Khayelitsha, on the Cape Flats, started life in the 1950s after the Group Areas Act was passed. It is one of the country's poorest urban centres.

8 Long Street

Affordable restaurants, trendy shops and a smattering of gay-friendly nightspots line Long Street, one of the liveliest and most integrated parts of the city. It is the hub of the city's backpacker scene (see p71).

Quirky shops and cafés on Long Street

9 Bo-Kaap Museum
MAP P4 ■ 71 Wale St, Bo-Kaap ■ 021 481 3938 ■ Open 10am–5pm Mon–Sat ■ Adm ■ www.iziko.org.za

This museum explores the evolution of the Bo-Kaap – an Islamic suburb that has been inhabited by the Cape Malay people since the abolition of slavery in the 1830s.

10 Imizamo Yethu

This recent township is set on the slopes above Hout Bay. The welcoming atmosphere makes up for the primitive conditions. Tours are provided by the residents (see p85).

TOP 10 SLANG WORDS AND PHRASES

Lekkers, or sweets (candies)

1 Ag!
Pronounced "Ach", and meaning "Oh man", this can be an expression of distaste (ag, sis!), sympathy (ag, shame!) or annoyance (ag, no!).

2 Bru
Derived from the Afrikaans *broer* (brother), this is a generic term of male address, a bit like "dude" in the USA or "mate" in the UK.

3 Dop
An alcoholic beverage – or drinking one (as in "let's have a quick dop").

4 Babalas
A Cape Coloureds (see p68) term for a hangover.

5 Just Now
This misleading phrase, which frequently confuses and amuses visitors to Cape Town, means "a bit later" – or "much later"!

6 Now Now
This expression of urgency means that something will happen much sooner than "just now". It does not, however, mean "now".

7 Izit?
Literally "is it", this is often interjected when another person speaks. It is similar to the English "really?"

8 Moerse
Very – as in "it's moerse cold", on a chilly day. Used to emphasize something.

9 Lekker
Good or nice (as in "we had a lekker time"). It can also mean that something is tasty. Sweets (candies) are called *lekkers* in Afrikaans.

10 Jol
The word means party or any good time, and is used both as a noun ("where's the jol?") or a verb ("let's jol").

🔟 Parks and Reserves

① Jonkershoek and Assegaaibosch Nature Reserves

A ramblers' paradise, these adjoining reserves protect the Jonkershoek Mountains, which rise 1,526 m (5,005 ft) on the eastern outskirts of Stellenbosch. Apart from the wildlife and montane *fynbos*, they also offer day walks, ranging from a stroll through the Assegaaibosch wild-flower garden, to the challenging 18-km (11-mile) Swartboskloof Trail *(see pp90–91)*.

② Cederberg Wilderness Area

About a 3-hour drive north of Cape Town, the rugged Cederberg is a dream for hikers, rock climbers, mountain bikers, photographers and stargazers. Day hikes visit marvellous russet-coloured sandstone rock formations, and there are some well-equipped camp sites and cottages for overnight stays *(see p102)*.

Rocky outcrops at Cederberg

③ Harold Porter National Botanical Garden

This botanical garden in Betty's Bay is an excellent place to see *fynbos* flora, including the *Disa uniflora* in its natural habitat, proteas, ericas and restios. The birdlife found in the garden is an added attraction for avid bird-watchers, with most *fynbos* endemics well represented *(see p104)*.

Pelicans at Table Bay Nature Reserve

④ Table Bay Nature Reserve

MAP B2 ▪ Grey Ave, Table View ▪ 021 444 0315 ▪ Open 7:30am–5:30pm daily ▪ Adm ▪ www.friendsofrietvlei.co.za

Located in suburban Milnerton and Table View, this reserve is one of the top bird-watching sites in Cape Town and it provides protection to the Diep River floodplain, which attracts freshwater and marine birds. Almost 200 species have been recorded to date. Between October and March, there is an influx of migrant waders.

⑤ Silvermine

MAP H3 ▪ 021 789 2457 ▪ Open May–Aug: 8am–5pm; Sep–Apr: 7am–6pm ▪ Adm ▪ www.sanparks.org

Part of the central section of Table Mountain National Park, Silvermine is a refreshing alternative to the Table Mountain massif. The Silvermine River Walk provides an introduction to *fynbos* vegetation and birdlife, while the steeper walk to Noordhoek Peak and Elephant's Eye Cave offers spectacular oceanic views.

⑥ Kogelberg Biosphere Reserve

Just 100 km (62 miles) from Cape Town, the craggy mountains of the Kogelberg feel like true wilderness. Book an eco-friendly cabin well in advance or visit on a day trip to kayak the river, hike mountain trails and spot the wild horses *(see p104)*.

⑦ West Coast National Park

Centred on the sheltered Langebaan Lagoon, this marine park is popular with bird and watersport enthusiasts. Apart from the coastal scenery, attractions include wildlife such as eland, bontebok and springbok. Visit in August and September, when the blooming wild flowers in the Postberg section are a magnificent sight *(see p101)*.

⑧ Paarl Mountain Nature Reserve

MAP E1 ▪ Jan Phillips Mountain Dr, Paarl ▪ 082 744 5900 ▪ Open Apr–Sep: 7am–6pm daily; Oct–Mar: 7am–7pm daily ▪ Adm

Situated on the outskirts of Paarl, with a mix of montane *fynbos* and indigenous forests, this reserve protects the granite domes, which give the town its name. This reserve is a great place for a bracing walk, and is also popular with anglers and mountain bikers.

⑨ Kirstenbosch National Botanical Garden

On the eastern slopes of Table Mountain, these landscaped gardens showcase South Africa's peerless indigenous plant varieties, and can be explored on a network of well-maintained, mostly wheelchair-friendly footpaths *(see pp26–7)*.

⑩ Table Mountain National Park

MAP T4 ▪ 021 712 0527 ▪ Opening hrs vary for each section ▪ Adm for select sections ▪ www.sanparks.org

Proclaimed as a national park in 1998, this urban park extends from Signal Hill in the north to Cape Point at the tip of the Cape Peninsula *(see pp32–3)*. This rich biodiversity, with an estimated 2,200 plant species and fauna ranging from Chacma baboons and rock hyraxes (dassies) to endemic birds and frogs, thrives within metropolitan Cape Town.

Hikers in Table Mountain National Park

TOP10 Wildlife Experiences

Pelicans at Rondevlei Nature Reserve

1 Bird-watching, Rondevlei Nature Reserve

This large wetland on the Cape Flats is easily the best place to spot water-birds in suburban Cape Town. Among the 230 species recorded here are the great white pelican, African spoonbill and various herons *(see p85)*.

2 Harbour Cruise

City Sightseeing Harbour Cruise: departs from Two Oceans Aquarium, Dock Rd; 0861 733 287; daily (see website for times); www. citysightseeing.co.za ▪ Waterfront Charters: departs from Quay 5; 021 418 3168; 9am–7pm daily; www.waterfrontcharters.co.za

Operators on the V&A Waterfront offer cruises through the harbour with a near certainty of sighting Cape fur seals, gulls and terns. On longer cruises out to Table

Bay you might also catch sight of dolphins or whales.

3 Penguin Colony, Boulders Beach

Waddling around like tipsy tuxedoed waiters, these flightless birds are a firm fixture on the tourist itinerary. Amazingly, the 2,000-strong Boulder colony was founded by two breeding pairs in 1982 *(see pp30–31)*.

4 Scuba Diving and Snorkelling

The kelp forests and tidal pools of the Atlantic offer excellent opportunities for diving to glimpse weird and wonderful marine creatures *(see pp52–3)*.

5 Land-Based Whale Watching

Peak season: Jun–Nov; calving season: Jul–Aug

The Western Cape has the world's best land-based whale watching. Cliffs at Hermanus, De Hoop and False Bay offer great vantage points to view the southern right whale breaching in deep, sheltered bays *(see pp32–3 & 101–3)*.

6 Duiker Island, Near Hout Bay

A flat granite outcrop 6 km (4 miles) offshore, this island supports a 5,000–6,000 strong colony of seals, three species of cormorant and some penguins. Boat tours run past the seal-lined shores *(see p86)*.

Colony of seals at Duiker Island

7 Inverdoorn Game Reserve

A spectacular sight in the Karoo, Inverdoorn Game Reserve is only a few hours' drive from Cape Town. It is rich in wildlife, including lion, cheetah, giraffe, antelope and white rhino. A range of leisure activities are also available *(see p72)*.

8 Cape of Good Hope

The most southerly sector of Table Mountain National Park, the Cape of Good Hope boasts spectacular oceanic viewpoints. It also offers great wildlife watching – bontebok, grysbok and mountain zebra coexist with the Chacma baboon, eland and small grey mongoose *(see pp32–3)*.

Baboons at the Cape of Good Hope

9 Dassies on Table Mountain

Cute, semi-tame dassies (rock hyraxes) sunbathe on Table Mountain. Resembling guinea pigs, but larger and sharper-toothed, these oddball creatures are dwarfish relics of a group of ungulates that dominated the African herbivore niche about 35 million years ago *(see pp22–3)*.

10 Aquila Private Game Reserve

R46, Touws River (off the N1) ▪ 021 430 7260 ▪ www.aquilasafari.com

Inhabited by large animals including lion, elephant and buffalo, this reserve in the southern Karoo offers a wide variety of activities including day safaris from Cape Town, horseback and quad-bike adventures, and overnight and fly-in options.

TOP 10 ENDEMIC FLORA AND FAUNA

The distinctive king protea bloom

1 King Protea
This pineapple-sized salmon-pink bloom is South Africa's national flower.

2 Red Disa
The "Pride of Table Mountain", this very pretty red flower blooms in December and January.

3 Silver Tree
Restricted to the Cape Peninsula, this attractive protea-affiliated tree has silver-haired stems and cone-like flowers.

4 African Penguin
The only penguin that breeds in South Africa. Two other sub-Antarctic species sometimes turn up on Cape beaches.

5 Bontebok
This beautifully marked antelope was on the verge of extinction in the early 20th century, but the species has since recovered *(see p102)*.

6 Cape Dwarf Chameleon
The most readily observed of four chameleon species living in the Western Cape mountains.

7 Cape Mountain Zebra
Rescued from extinction, the Cape Mountain Zebra has fared better than its close relative, the quagga, which was hunted out in the 19th century.

8 Cape Sugarbird
This long-tailed *fynbos* dweller belongs to a family whose range is limited to South Africa and Zimbabwe.

9 Orange-Breasted Sunbird
A dazzling nectar-eater that only lives in flowering *fynbos* habitats.

10 Table Mountain Ghost Frog
This club-fingered frog is restricted to several streams on the eastern and southern slopes of the mountain.

🔟 Viewpoints

View of the Lion's Head and Central Cape Town from Signal Hill

1 Signal Hill

Accessible by car or foot and rising between the City Bowl and Sea Point, the flat-topped 350-m (1,148-ft) Signal Hill is an extension of a taller, hornlike rock formation known as Lion's Head. From Signal Hill Road, viewpoints overlook the eastern side of the city, while the picnic site at the top affords a stunning view over the Atlantic Seaboard and Table Bay. It is one of the best-loved spots in Cape Town to watch a sunset in the red western sky (see p70).

2 Rhodes Memorial

Situated on the eastern slopes of Table Mountain, this is a rather bombastic memorial to the former Cape Prime Minister. The views over the Cape Flats to distant Helderberg and the Hottentots Holland Mountains are best enjoyed from the adjacent restaurant (see p78).

Rhodes Memorial

3 Rooikrans

In the far south of the Table Mountain National Park, this underutilized viewpoint provides a thrilling north-facing vantage over the False Bay seaboard. There are also great whale-watching opportunities between June and November (see p32).

4 Chapman's Peak Drive

One of the world's most spectacular marine drives, this toll road was constructed in 1915–22 along the band of shale that divides the granite base of Chapman's Peak from the overlying sandstone. It winds along the mountainside between Hout Bay and Noordhoek with viewpoints along the way. Stop to admire the sheer cliffs of Chapman's Peak and the Atlantic battering the shore below *(see p86)*.

5 Tokara Wine Estate

At the crest of Helshoogte Pass, this wine and olive estate boasts perhaps the most scenic location in the Winelands. The views stretch across eucalyptus-swathed slopes to False Bay and – on a clear day – distant Table Mountain. Best enjoyed with a chilled glass of one of the estate's crisp Sauvignon Blanc wines *(see p36)*.

6 Franschhoek Pass
MAP F2

This pass is often ignored by tourists in the Winelands because it leads to remote Villiersdorp rather than trendy Stellenbosch. But it is worth following this road for a couple of kilometres to take in the lovely views over the thatched rooftops and the expansive vineyards that are located in the Franschhoek Valley *(see pp36–7)*.

7 Bloubergstrand
MAP B2

About 10 km (6 miles) north of Cape Town, the Bloubergstrand beach hems in Table Bay on the West Coast. This "Blue Mountain Beach" is named after the flat-topped Table Mountain, which looms over its sandy expanse. Usually at its prettiest in the morning, the beach is also a lovely place to visit in the afternoon, when you can enjoy the vista from its alfresco cafés.

Kitesurfers on Bloubergstrand beach

8 Cape Point

Situated at the southern tip of the Cape Peninsula within the Cape of Good Hope, Cape Point is reached via a steep footpath or a chuffing funicular. The views include Atlantic-battered cliffs and beaches and an open seascape that stretches all the way south to Antarctica *(see pp32–3)*.

The sea-worn cliffs at Cape Point

9 Table Mountain Upper Cableway

Within 15 minutes of the Upper Cableway station, a succession of viewpoints reveal the geography of the Western Cape, from nearby Signal Hill to surf-splashed Robben Island and False Bay, all overshadowed by the Hottentots Holland Mountains. No less impressive are the views across the Cape Peninsula's mountainous spine to Cape Point *(see pp22–3)*.

10 Clarence Drive
MAP D4–5

Hugging the cliffy coast between Gordon's Bay and Rooi-Els, Clarence Drive is one of the most spectacularly beautiful roads in South Africa, and, luckily, viewpoints abound. Look out, too, for baboons along the way.

🔟 Beaches

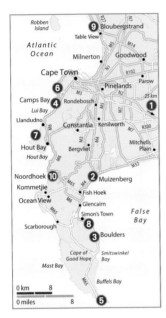

make it very popular with families. If the sunbathing gets too monotonous, there are also some great tidal rock pools at Gordon's Bay.

2 Muizenberg

On the northern shore of False Bay, Muizenberg was Cape Town's trendiest beach in the 1960s, but its glitz has now faded. Still, it is usually safe for swimming and excellent for surfing. Facilities include a protected pool, waterslides, mini-golf, snack shops and colourful beach huts, and the beach remains a favourite with families. It is very accessible by train from the city centre (see p85).

Colourful Muizenberg beach huts

1 Bikini Beach, Gordon's Bay

MAP D4

Less than an hour's drive east of Cape Town, secluded Bikini Beach is the most popular of the many beaches around Strand. Overlooked by the Helderberg Mountains, it offers clear views across False Bay. The shallow waters are safe for swimming, and an abundance of restaurants and cafés

3 Boulders Beach

This is a lovely, secluded beach on the southern fringe of the penguin colony. Enjoy the company of these remarkable birds, who bustle fearlessly around the same rocks where tourists sunbathe. An entrance fee is required (see p30).

Penguins at Boulders Beach

View over Camps Bay beach

4 Camps Bay

Overlooked by the spectacular Twelve Apostles formation on the western face of Table Mountain, this wide, sandy beach lies alongside the main road through Camps Bay, below a row of street cafés, restaurants and bars. Popular with families over the holidays, it is quieter at other times. Deckchairs and parasols are available for hire (see p68).

5 Cape of Good Hope

Set below Cape Point, this windswept beach is arguably the most beautiful on the peninsula. As well as attracting sunbathers and swimmers, the Cape is also a magnet for walkers and nature enthusiasts (see pp32–3).

6 Clifton Beach

Within very easy walking distance of Sea Point and Green Point, perennially fashionable Clifton is the closest swimming beach to the city centre. Of the four sandy coves, divided by granite outcrops, Fourth Beach has the best facilities, including changing rooms, public toilets, snack and soda kiosks. Deck chairs and umbrellas are available for rental. The waters are chilly and the undertow should not be underestimated (see p70).

7 Sandy Bay
MAP G2

Protected by high dunes and dotted with secluded rocky coves for sunbathing, Sandy Bay near Llandudno has long been a semi-official nudist beach. It also hosts something of a gay scene, although by no means exclusively so. It is not accessible by public transport, and is often too chilly for swimming.

8 Seaforth Beach

Like nearby Boulders, this beach, within walking distance of Simon's Town, is hemmed in by gigantic rocks. Generally, it is not too busy, and there's a chance of spotting stray penguins waddling past. The charming Seaforth Restaurant with its wooden balcony overlooks the beach (see p31).

9 Bloubergstrand

The *blouberg* (blue mountain) is Table Mountain (see pp22–3), whose flat-topped profile is displayed in full glory on a clear day. Sandy for the most part, Bloubergstrand has enough rocky protrusions to keep it interesting. Rather exposed in windy weather, the beach is a favourite for watersports (see p49).

10 Noordhoek

Below spectacular Chapman's Peak (see p86), Noordhoek is a seemingly endless arc of glorious white sand near Kommetjie. Although too exposed to the elements to host much of a beach scene, it attracts walkers, bird-watchers and horse riders. Perfect for a long seaside stroll (see p87).

Horse riding at Noordhoek

🔟 Adventure Activities

A rock climber in the Western Cape

weather permits. You can book a flight at the heliport on the V&A Waterfront.

3 Caving
Cape Peninsula Spelaeological Society (CPSS): 021 701 0841; www.cpss.caving.org.za

The network of sandstone caverns above Kalk Bay is reached via a steep footpath offering breathtaking views over False Bay. The earliest evidence of human habitation at the Cape was excavated here. Some clambering and crawling is required to explore the cavernous depths. Do carry a torch.

1 Rock Climbing
City Rock: 021 447 1326; call ahead to book; www.cityrock.co.za

The craggy Western Cape peaks are a rock-climber's paradise. City Rock is the leading centre to visit for a good selection of climbing gear or experienced instructors. It also has an indoor climbing centre.

4 Kitesurfing
Cabrinha: 021 554 1729; www.cabrinha.co.za

Cape Town is known for its windy weather, which, along with the might of the Atlantic Ocean, makes for perfect kitesurfing. There's always a group of kitesurfers at the eastern end of Muizenberg beach, but the best locations are the Table View area and, further north, the West Coast. Langebaan Lagoon is great for beginners.

2 Helicopter Rides
Sport Helicopters: 021 419 5907; www.sporthelicopters.co.za

There is no more thrilling a way of seeing the Cape Peninsula and Table Mountain than from the air, when

5 Scuba Diving
Scuba Shack: 072 603 8630; www.scubashack.co.za

The coast to the north of Durban is renowned for its offshore reefs teeming with colourful fish. However,

Helicopter ride over Table Mountain

Scuba diving in waters off Cape Town

8 Abseiling
Abseil Africa: 021 424 4760; www.abseilafrica.co.za

For spectacular heart-stopping views from Table Mountain, take in Abseil Africa's 112-m (367-ft) controlled descent of the western face. It is considered the world's highest commercial abseil.

9 Quad Biking
Downhill Adventures: 021 422 0388; www.downhilladventures.com

The natural beauty in and around Cape Town makes it a great place for quad biking. Experienced guides will show you how to operate the bike before taking you on an exciting ride through the many tracks and trails across the Cape Peninsula and the Winelands.

10 Paragliding
Para-Pax: 082 881 4724; www.parapax.co.za

Signal Hill and Lion's Head are spectacular locations for tandem paragliding, offering stunning views of Cape Town's Atlantic Seaboard suburbs, the V&A Waterfront and Table Bay. No prior experience is required for the enjoyable 20- to 30-minute glide as you are clipped into the pilot's harness.

the chillier waters off Cape Town also provide great diving possibilities – immense forests of swaying kelp, friendly seals on the Atlantic Seaboard, and a large number of shipwrecks to be explored.

6 Winelands Ballooning
021 863 3192; runs Nov–Apr only, weather permitting; www.kapinfo.com

A blissful way to start the day is to glide serenely over the beautiful winelands around Paarl in a hot-air balloon. Leave at sunrise, letting the wind (and your expert pilot) navigate the balloon until you land, from where a support vehicle takes you back to Paarl for a champagne breakfast. Allow 4 to 5 hours for the whole experience.

Hot-air balloon

7 Kloofing
Absolute Adventures: 074 114 6831; www.absoluteadventures.co.za

Kloofing – also known as canyoning – is a uniquely Western Cape extreme adventure; you must always be on a guided excursion. It involves hiking, boulder-hopping, wading through fast-moving rivers and jumping into pools from cliffs up to 15 m (49 ft) high. The best sites such as the ominously named Suicide Gorge and Kamikaze Kanyon are in the mountains outside of the city.

Paragliding in Cape Town

🔟 Sports and Outdoor Activities

① Rugby

Newlands Stadium: MAP J2; 021 659 4600; www.wprugby.com

Traditionally one of the world's best teams, the South African "Springboks" have twice won the Rugby World Cup (in 1995 and 2007). International matches are held at Newlands Stadium, home to Western Province and the Stormers Super Rugby team.

Springboks playing rugby

② Football

Cape Town Stadium: MAP N1; www.capetown.gov.za/capetown stadium

Ajax Cape Town and Cape Town City FC represent the city in South Africa's Premier Soccer League. They play home matches at Cape Town Stadium.

③ Golf

Rondebosch Golf Club: MAP H1; 021 689 4176 ■ Steenberg Golf Club: MAP H3; 021 715 0227; www.steenberggolfclub.co.za

There are several golf courses in Cape Town. Two of the best are Rondebosch Golf Club and the Steenberg Golf Club.

④ Cricket

Newlands Cricket Stadium: MAP H2; 021 657 2050; www. newlandscricket.com

Newlands is one of the world's most beautiful cricket grounds with Table Mountain and Devil's Peak as a backdrop. It's home to the Western Cape's provincial team Cape Cobras, and regularly hosts One Day International, Twenty20 and Test matches.

⑤ Deep-Sea Fishing

Hooked on Africa: 021 790 5332; www.hookedonafrica.co.za ■ Big Blue Fishing Charters: 021 786 5667; www. bigbluefishingcharters.com

The waters off the Cape Peninsula are renowned for their great deep-sea fishing, with tuna being a speciality. Charters depart from the harbours at Hout Bay or Simon's Town.

⑥ Horse Riding, Noordhoek

Sleepy Hollow: 021 789 2341; www.sleepyhollowhorseriding.co.za

The sandy Noordhoek Beach below Chapman's Peak is great for horse riding. Lessons are available for all ages, as well as disabled riders.

⑦ Hiking

Ridgeway Ramblers: 082 522 6056; www.ridgwayramblers.co.za

Hiking trails suitable for all levels of fitness traverse most of the nature reserves and national parks. Most can be walked unguided, but there's also the option of going with an experienced guide.

Hikers looking down on Hout Bay

Mountain biking

TOP 10 SOUTH AFRICAN SPORTING ICONS

1 Ernie Els
The former world number-one golfer, better known as the Big Easy, has won four major titles.

2 Makhaya Ntini
South Africa's first black international cricketer reached No. 2 in world rankings for test bowlers in 2006.

3 Benni McCarthy
His 32 international goals while playing for the national team Bafana Bafana (1997–2012) are a South African record.

4 Francois Pienaar
He captained the South African rugby team, which won the 1995 Rugby World Cup on its home turf.

5 Shaun Pollock
This former national cricket captain was a top-ranked bowling all-rounder (416 wickets/3,781 runs in tests).

6 Caster Semenya
She won an Olympic gold medal at Rio 2016 for the women's 800-m race.

7 Penny Heyns
Winner of both the 100-m and 200-m breaststroke in the 1996 Olympics, Penny Heyns was the first ever woman to win gold in both races.

8 Mountain Biking
Downhill Adventures: 021 422 0388; www.downhilladventures.com
The mountainous Winelands offer great opportunities for cyclists. Bikes can be hired in all the main centres, and several reserves have trails.

9 Surfing
Gary's Surf School: Muizenberg; 021 788 9839; www.garysurf.co.za
The Western Cape offers some of the world's best surfing, with schools providing lessons and board and wet-suit hire. Muizenberg, on False Bay, is a reliable place to learn. Sites along the Atlantic seaboard, while less busy, are more challenging.

8 Lucas Radebe
Former South Africa and Leeds captain, he played in the football team that won the 1996 Africa Nations Cup.

9 Gary Player
One of the all-time golfing greats, Player is also known for designing golf courses in South Africa and around the world.

10 Roland Schoeman
Four-time member of the South African Olympics team (2000–2012), he broke nine swimming records during his career.

10 Kayaking in False Bay
Kayak Cape Town: 082 501 8930; www.kayakcapetown.co.za
Starting from Simon's Town, ideally on a windless day, paddle through scenic False Bay, and look for penguins, dolphins and whales.

Roland Schoeman in action

TOP 10 Children's Attractions

harp, logic puzzles and human gyroscope. There's a café serving light meals.

3 Monkey Town Primate Sanctuary

MAP D4 ▪ Mondeor Rd, Somerset West ▪ 021 858 1060 ▪ Open 8am–5pm daily ▪ www.monkeys.co.za

Most of the primates in this sanctuary have been rescued from captivity. The species, from chimps to pygmy marmosets, live in a large, green enclosure surrounded by a viewing walkway.

1 World of Birds

MAP G2 ▪ Valley Road, Hout Bay ▪ 021 790 2730 ▪ Open 9am–5pm daily ▪ Adm ▪ www.worldofbirds.org.za

Situated in Hout Bay, this is Africa's largest bird park with over 400 indigenous and exotic species, including parrots and barbets. Visitors can follow the stages of birdlife, right from eggs in incubation to the feeding of chicks.

4 Blue Train Park

MAP M1 ▪ Beach Road, Mouille Point ▪ 084 314 9200 ▪ Open May–Sep: 12:30pm–6pm Tue–Thu; Oct–Apr: 9:30am–6pm Tue–Sun ▪ Adm ▪ www.thebluetrainpark.co.za

There are all sorts of things to keep little ones entertained at this impressive outdoor park, including bouncy castles, jungle gyms, a mini bike track, a climbing wall and even a simulated ice-skating rink. The miniature train that gives the park its name makes constant loops around the edge of the park, with one ride per person included in the entrance fee.

World of Birds

The miniature train in Blue Train Park

2 Cape Town Science Centre

MAP H1 ▪ 370B Main Road, Observatory ▪ 021 300 3200 ▪ Open 9am–4:30pm Mon–Sat, 10am–4:30pm Sun ▪ Adm ▪ www.ctsc.org.za

This is the perfect place to head on a rainy day. There are more than 250 interactive exhibits to keep kids of all ages entertained. Little ones love the electric model train set and the chance to build a wall with foam bricks, while older kids (and adults) favour things such as the stringless

The beach section of the penguin exhibit at Two Oceans Aquarium

5 Two Oceans Aquarium

South Africa's leading aquarium has an extraordinary diversity of marine life from the Atlantic and the warmer Indian Ocean. The penguins, sharks and giant rays are favourites with children. A free activity centre hosts puppet shows and arts and crafts. Visit at feeding time (see p14).

6 Imhoff Farm

MAP G4 ■ Kommetjie ■ 021 783 4545 ■ Open 10am–5pm daily ■ www.imhofffarm.co.za

This restored 18th-century farm en route to Cape Point has domestic animals roaming the farmyard. There are also pony and camel rides.

7 Iziko Planetarium

The domed planetarium, part of the Iziko South African Museum complex in the Company's Garden, features daily shows introducing the brilliant southern night sky. There are also special shows for kids (see p13).

8 Wild Clover Farm

MAP D2 ■ R304, Stellenbosch ■ 021 865 2248 ■ Open 9am–5pm daily ■ www.wildclover.co.za

With little bikes, pony rides, archery and game drives to see antelope, zebra and giraffe, Wild Clover is one of the best places for families to take a break in the Winelands. For the grown-ups there's a microbrewery and a small winery, plus a restaurant and self-catering accommodation.

9 Spier Wine Farm

The most child-friendly of the Cape wine estates, Spier has a number of playgrounds and an exciting eagle-encounter programme with shows as well as the chance for encounters with Wahlberg's eagles and black eagles (see p92).

Child-friendly Spier Wine Farm

10 Giraffe House

MAP D2 ■ Cnr R304 (towards Stellenbosch) and R101 (towards Paarl) ■ 021 884 4506 ■ Open 9am–5pm daily ■ Adm ■ www. giraffehouse.co.za

Giraffe House provides easy access to some wonderful wildlife and bird species. Focusing on African wildlife, the sanctuary provides an amazing opportunity to enjoy a family picnic in the fresh air while experiencing and learning about animals and conservation. The species here include giraffe, zebra, eland, teals, bontebok, springbok, impala, lovebirds and parrots.

🔟 Wining and Dining

Exclusive dining in The Tasting Room at Le Quartier Français

1 The Tasting Room at Le Quartier Français

The Tasting Room is the place for a special occasion splurge. Diners sit down to an eight-course surprise feast showcasing local flavours and seasonal produce (see p99). For something a bit more casual, try the tapas menu in The Garden Room.

2 Den Anker Restaurant and Bar

Set on a small jetty, this is one of the Waterfront's top eateries, serving Belgian specialities, local seafood including West Coast crayfish and great European draft beers. Outdoor tables have a view of seals and boats in the harbour with Table Mountain as a backdrop (see p76).

3 La Colombe

At this elegant, first-class restaurant – rated as one of Cape Town's best – multi-course menus feature top-quality local ingredients that are given a French touch, with a dash of Asian fusion. Book early for a table on the balcony with forest and mountain views (see p81).

4 The Test Kitchen

This is widely considered the best restaurant on the continent. Plan months ahead if you want to sample the multi-course tasting menu. Tables at the sister restaurant, the Pot Luck Club, are easier to obtain (see p77).

5 Gold Restaurant

At the unabashedly touristy Gold Restaurant, you'll taste traditional delicacies from across Africa during a 14-course banquet. Music and dance accompanies your meal, and you are even scattered with 24-carat gold dust before you leave (see p77).

6 Terroir

Classic pairings can make dishes appear simple, but the chef at this establishment knows how to bring out the flavours of the seasonal produce. Take your cue from the slow cooking methods and make it a long dining experience, enhanced by estate wines (see p98).

Terroir's elegant cuisine

7 Jordan Restaurant

Contemporary dishes feature local meats and seafood, such as springbok and West Coast mussels, and renowned chef George Jardine changes the seasonal menu daily. Vast windows maximize the views of the dam, surrounding vineyards and dramatic mountains *(see p98)*.

8 Savoy Cabbage

This is one of Cape Town's trendiest eateries, set in a restored Victorian building in the city centre. The historic setting is offset by a funky interior, and the imaginative menu is strong on game, shellfish and vegetarian dishes *(see p77)*.

Spacious interior of Savoy Cabbage

9 The Foodbarn

Many of Cape Town's best chefs cite Franck Dangereux – owner and chef of The Foodbarn – as their mentor, after his previous work at La Colombe. Expect superb French-influenced food, sublime sauces and boutique wines by the carafe, in the farm village of Noordhoek *(see p89)*.

10 Picnics at Boschendal

Something about the Winelands invites lingering picnics with chilled white wine. No estate offers this with as much panache as Boschendal, where you can enjoy local artisanal goodies in one of two super-scenic picnic spots *(see p36)*.

TOP 10 SOUTH AFRICAN DISHES AND DELICACIES

Cape Malay bobotie

1 Bobotie
A Cape Malay classic of minced beef and yellow rice, sweetened by raisins and topped with an egg sauce.

2 Potjiekos
This dish features meat and vegetables cooked slowly in a *potjie* (a cast-iron black pot) over an open fire.

3 Waterblommetjie Bredie
A Cape stew made of lamb and *waterblommetjie*, a water plant that resembles an artichoke.

4 Tomato Bredie
A thick, tasty tomato-based stew made of succulent Karoo lamb.

5 Boerewors
Spicy, fatty "farmer's sausage", best *braaied* (barbecued) on an open fire.

6 Malva Pudding
This sweet, spongy Dutch pudding contains apricot jam and is served hot.

7 Melktert
This dish is a milkier and sweeter version of a custard tart. Dates back to Cape Malay-Dutch cooking.

8 Biltong
Spicy strips of dried, salted and spiced raw beef or game, biltong is reminiscent of beef jerky.

9 Pap 'n' Stew
The traditional staple in most of South Africa, this is a meat stew that is eaten along with *mealie pap* (a porridge made from ground maize).

10 Koeksisters
Translated as "cake sisters", these are doughnut-like spiral pastries with a sticky-sweet coating.

Koeksisters

For a key to restaurant price ranges see p77

🔟 Cape Town and the Winelands for Free

Views from Oranjezicht City Farm

1 Oranjezicht City Farm

MAP P6 ▪ Upper Orange Street, Oranjezicht, Cape Town ▪ 083 508 1066 ▪ Open 8am–4pm Mon–Fri, 8am–1pm Sat ▪ www.ozcf.co.za

Located on the site of a historic farm, this non-profit urban farm on the slopes of Table Mountain is a joy to explore. Guided tours are available for a small donation. The farm's organic market takes place between 9am and 2pm each Saturday at Granger Bay.

2 Rhodes Memorial

The ostentatious memorial on the slopes of Devil's Peak was built in 1912 to honour the Cape Colony's one-time Prime Minister, Cecil John Rhodes, who also founded Rhodesia. Whether you approve of his politics or not, there's a great view across the Cape Flats and on to the Hottentots Holland Mountains (see p78).

3 Company's Garden

There's plenty to see for free in this glorious city park, including an aviary, the 18th-century façade of the president's official Cape Town residence, and a range of monuments and memorials (see pp12–13).

4 Coastal Walk from Muizenberg to Kalk Bay

The 3-km (2-mile) walk from Muizenberg's Edwardian train station to Kalk Bay hugs the coast. Take a dip in the tidal pool at St James; browse Kalk Bay's galleries and shops; and end up at the harbour, where fishermen and seals vie for the same rewards (see pp85 & 87).

5 City Walking Tours

City Sightseeing: 0861 733 287; www.citysightseeing.co.za

The company in charge of open-top bus trips also offers free 90-minute walking tours taking in historically significant neighbourhoods. Amble through District Six, wander the colourful houses of the Bo-Kaap or take a city centre stroll visiting Greenmarket Square and City Hall.

6 Climbing Lion's Head

MAP K6

You don't need money to get to the top of Lion's Head, but you do need a head for heights. The peak is 669-m- (2,195-ft-) high, and the 2-hour round-trip hike is strenuous, involving chains and ladders. Join the locals for a full-moon night hike.

Rhodes Memorial

7 The Noon Gun

Clamber up Signal from Bo-Kaap Hill and take your place behind the safety line to witness this cannon herald the arrival of noon. It has been fired each day except Sunday since 1806, and there has only been one recorded instance of both main and backup gun failing.

8 Green Point Urban Park

A stone's throw from the ocean, this park is a magnificent place to wander, cycle or picnic in. You can admire indigenous plants and modern sculptures, get lost in the labyrinth and indulge in a little bird-watching. There's a superb playground for children and an outdoor gym for the grown-ups (see p70).

Green Point Urban Park

9 Woodstock Street Art
MAP H1

This once run-down industrial district is now a creative hub filled with galleries, quirky boutiques, craft breweries and micro-distilleries. Woodstock is also home to an eclectic collection of murals featuring political, cultural and environmental messages.

10 Parliament Tours
MAP Q5 ▪ 100 Plein Street, Cape Town ▪ 021 403 2266 ▪ Open 9am–noon Mon–Fri (tours hourly) ▪ www.parliament.gov.za

Learn all about the history of South Africa's parliament on an hour-long tour. Be sure to book in advance and bring your passport along on the day.

TOP 10 MONEY-SAVING TIPS

Free waterfront entertainment

1 Visit in winter (May to August) for discounts on accommodation, transport and attractions.

2 GoCards offer passes giving discounted or free entry to a number of attractions. www.gocards.co.za

3 EatOut keeps an up-to-date list of daily restaurant specials around the city. www.eatout.co.za

4 Look out for free concerts at the V&A Waterfront year-round and in De Waal Park throughout summer.

5 Many wineries offer tastings for a nominal fee, with no pressure to buy.

6 Most of Cape Town's museums offer free entry on certain commemorative days. Iziko has a complete list. www.iziko.org.za

7 The MyCiti bus to Hout Bay is an equally scenic, cheaper alternative to the open-top City Sightseeing bus.

8 Keep hold of receipts – non-South Africans can claim VAT back.

9 Grab a free copy of *Coast to Coast*, a budget travel guide offering discounts.

10 Book online for attractions where possible – there's often a discount.

South African wine tasting

⓽10 Festivals and Events

Musicians rocking the Cape Town International Jazz Festival

① Kaapse Klopse
2 Jan

Also known as the Cape Minstrel Festival, this colourful New Year's welcome originated as a response by former slaves to an 1848 visit by "blackfaces" (white American minstrels who blackened their faces with burnt cork). Local people paint their faces white and march through Cape Town.

② Maynardville Open-Air Theatre
MAP H2 ▪ Maynardville Park, Wynberg ▪ Jan–Feb ▪ www.artscape.co.za/maynardville-open-air-theatre

This 700-seat open-air theatre has hosted a Shakespeare-in-the-Park Festival since 1956. It attracts up to 20,000 patrons annually.

Festivalgoers at Kaapse Klopse

③ Stellenbosch Wine Festival
MAP D2 ▪ 021 886 4330 ▪ Feb ▪ www.stellenboschwinefestival.co.za

Wine-lovers descend on Stellenbosch for this three-day event that features more than 500 wines by Cape estates. The festival includes wine-tasting tutorials, craft workshops, gourmet food and kids' entertainment.

④ Cape Town International Jazz Festival
021 671 0506 ▪ Mar last weekend ▪ www.capetownjazzfest.com

Hosted at the Cape Town International Convention Centre (CTICC) on five indoor and outdoor stages over two nights, the continent's largest jazz festival attracts more than 40 top local and international performers.

⑤ Cape Town Pride Festival
Feb–March ▪ www.capetownpride.org

Cape Town's most important gay festival was inaugurated in 2001. Pride Parade Day attracts a stream of colourful floats and involves drag shows, fashion events and an after party. Other events in the two-week festival include pageants, balls, tea parties and gay movies.

⑥ Cape Town Festival
021 465 9042 ▪ Mar/Apr ▪ www.capetownfestival.co.za

This arts festival began in 1999 to promote integration and celebrate the multiracial communities of Cape Town. It is held in March or April in the Company's Garden (see pp12–13).

Cape Town Festival of Beer

Late Nov ▪ www.capetownfestival
ofbeer.co.za

A three-day event at which microbrewers from across the country join with major brands to offer their wares to a thirsty public.

Franschhoek Cap Classique and Champagne Festival

MAP F2 ▪ **Early Dec** ▪ www.
franschhoekmcc.co.za

Celebrate the superb local wines made with the Champagne method at this event held at the Huguenot Monument. Top restaurants create dishes to pair with the bubbles.

Kirstenbosch Summer Sunset Concerts

MAP H2 ▪ Rhodes Drive, Newlands ▪ 021 799 8783 ▪ **Nov–Apr** ▪ www.
sanbi.org/events/kirstenbosch

A wonderful way to enjoy a Sunday sunset. The open-air concerts appeal to all musical tastes and take place within the beautiful botanic gardens.

Kirstenbosch Summer Sunset Concerts

Oude Libertas Summer Season Festival

MAP D2 ▪ Stellenbosch ▪ 021 809 7380 ▪ **Jan–Mar** ▪ www.oudelibertas.co.za

This music festival is held at the Oude Libertas Estate on the Papegaaiberg. It has an eclectic programme featuring traditional chamber music, jazz and *boeremusiek* (Afrikaans folk).

TOP 10 SPORTING EVENTS

Racers at ABSA Cape Epic

1 ABSA Cape Epic
A two-person team event featuring seven days of off-road mountain-bike racing through the Winelands in March.

2 Cape Town Cycle Tour
South Africa's largest individually timed cycling race, this attracts 35,000 on a 109-km (68-mile) route in March.

3 Old Mutual Two Oceans Marathon
This 56-km (35-mile) ultra-marathon, reputed as the most beautiful in the world, takes place over Easter Weekend.

4 Discovery World Triathlon Cape Town
Attracting professional and novice athletes over two days in March, this is part of the World Triathlon Series.

5 L'Ormarins Queen's Plate
These horse races at Kenilworth Racecourse in January include hospitality events and fashion contests.

6 The Colour Run
This 5-km (3-mile) run in November is all about getting doused in coloured powder and the parties at the end.

7 Twilight Festival
A run/walk/skate in fancy-dress for 4 km (2 miles) in early December in the city centre. Raises money for charity.

8 J&B Metropolitan Handicap
Held at the end of January at Kenilworth Racecourse, this high-profile event is a mix of fashion and horse-racing.

9 Cape Town 10s
Hosted over three days in February at Hamilton's Rugby Club, this tournament offers live music and beer tents.

10 Three Peaks Challenge
A mountain running challenge ascending Devil's Peak, Table Mountain and Lion's Head. Held in November.

Cape Town and the Winelands Area by Area

Spectacular view of Cape Bay and
Table Mountain from Bloubergstrand

TOP 10 Central Cape Town

The historic heart of South Africa's oldest city is bound by Table Bay to the north and Table Mountain to the south. Signal Hill forms an imposing barrier between the City Bowl's inner city suburbs and those along the Atlantic. Cape Town's historic buildings, museums, theatres, restaurants and clubs, together with a buzzing street life, confirm the city's status as one of Africa's major cultural centres.

View over Cape Town

CENTRAL CAPE TOWN

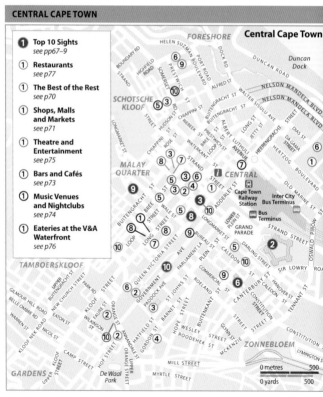

Central Cape Town

1. **Top 10 Sights**
   see pp67–9
1. **Restaurants**
   see p77
1. **The Best of the Rest**
   see p70
1. **Shops, Malls and Markets**
   see p71
1. **Theatre and Entertainment**
   see p75
1. **Bars and Cafés**
   see p73
1. **Music Venues and Nightclubs**
   see p74
1. **Eateries at the V&A Waterfront**
   see p76

1 Table Mountain

The 1,067-m (3,500-ft) high plateau of Table Mountain is reached by a rotating cablecar that offers 360° views across the city centre to the distant Hottentots Holland Mountains. At the top, a network of footpaths allows hikers to explore the *fynbos* vegetation. Maclear's Beacon, the highest summit, is less than an hour from the Upper Cableway Station. The more adventurous traveller might like to try Abseil Africa's controlled 112-m (367-ft) descent from a ledge over-looking Camps Bay *(see pp22–3)*.

2 Castle of Good Hope

Constructed in Table Bay between 1666 and 1679, Cape Town's oldest building – and a superbly

Guards at the Castle of Good Hope

preserved example of a Dutch East India Company fort – now stands inland as a result of land reclamation. An imposing slate and sandstone pentagon, it has a rather utilitarian design that is alleviated by the sculpted masonry on the bell tower and the Anton Anreith bas-relief above the Kat Balcony. An interesting military museum and Dr William Fehr's Cape-based art collection are also housed here *(see pp20–21)*.

3 Greenmarket Square
MAP P4

This cobbled square in the heart of old Cape Town served as a slave market under the Dutch East India Company (VOC; *see p40*), but its name alludes to its subsequent use as a fruit and vegetable market, which made way for a parking lot in the 1950s. Surrounded by historic buildings, many housing smart cafés and eateries, it is now home to a popular pan-African craft market and lively street performers.

Locals relax in Greenmarket Square

5 V&A Waterfront

Victoria Wharf Shopping Centre (5)

Victoria Basin

DOCK RD

PORTSWOOD RD ROAD

BEACH RD

Alfred Mall

Swing Bridge

Alfred Basin

Nelson Mandela Gateway

CLOCK TOWER PRECINCT

DOCK ROAD

The Watershed

WEST QUAY ROAD

Two Oceans Aquarium

New Marina

0 metres 200
0 yards 200

Table Mountain

↖ *Robben Island (13 km)*

GREEN POINT

See V&A Waterfront map, above

Beach Road

PAARDEN EILAND

Signal Hill

See Central Cape Town map

SEA POINT

N1

SALT RIVER

CLIFTON

M62

ORANJEZICHT

Camps Bay

ROSEBANK

N2

M3

Table Mountain

0 km 2
0 miles 2

BAKOVEN

4 Beach Road
MAP K3

Passing west of the city centre through the suburbs of Green Point and Sea Point, Beach Road runs along an attractive stretch of Atlantic coastline. The road is separated from the sea by a grassy promenade, where locals relax, jog and walk their dogs. It's great for a wander, especially at sunset. Don't miss the Green Point Lighthouse, the oldest in the country.

THE KHOISAN

When van Riebeeck established Cape Town in 1652 (see p40), the Western Cape had been inhabited by the Khoisan-speaking populace for several millennia. Within 200 years they were gone; some had fallen victim to diseases, while others were killed by gun-toting settlers. Those who remained integrated into the mixed-race community, Cape Coloureds.

Green Point Lighthouse, Beach Road

5 V&A Waterfront

Cape Town's reconstituted harbour is also the city's foremost shopping venue. Hundreds of shops, ranging from chain stores to quirky craft stalls, can be found alongside many restaurants and a host of tourist spots, including the Nelson Mandela Gateway. Boat and helicopter tour operators offer harbour cruises and flights over Table Mountain (see pp14–15).

6 District Six Museum

This moving tribute to District Six, bulldozed in the apartheid era (see p40), is housed in the former Buitenkant Methodist Church, whose association with the anti-apartheid movement led to its forced closure in 1988. The museum's centrepiece is a vast, annotated floor map of the suburb in its multiracial heyday. Other exhibits tell of the cruelty and destructiveness of the racism that dominated South African life for almost half a century (see pp18–19).

7 Camps Bay
MAP G1

Wonderfully set between mountain and sea, Camps Bay is where suburban Cape Town's Atlantic Seaboard gives way to the unspoilt coastal scenery of the Cape Peninsula. This idyllic suburb boasts one of the nicest beaches in greater Cape Town and has a fine range of restaurants and bars located on its waterfront.

The magnificent Camps Bay, set on the Atlantic coast

8 Michaelis Collection
MAP P4 ▪ Greenmarket Square ▪ 021 481 3933 ▪ Open 10am–5pm Mon–Sat ▪ Adm ▪ www.iziko.org.za

This world-renowned collection of paintings by Dutch and Flemish masters of the Golden Age (16th–18th centuries) was donated to the city by Sir Max Michaelis in 1914. Housed in the beautifully restored Old Townhouse, which served as the City Hall until 1905, the structure is counted among the foremost architectural gems of the city, and is a fabulous example of the early Cape Rococo style with its graceful triple-arched portico and pretty belfry.

Bo-Kaap's colourful houses

9 Bo-Kaap
MAP P4

The spiritual home of the Cape Malay community, Bo-Kaap (Upper Cape) is a vibrant neighbourhood in the city centre. Best known for its endlessly photogenic colourful houses, the area also has a small but interesting museum *(see p43)*. The best thing to do here, though, is to eat traditional Cape Malay cuisine. Seek out the local version of *koeksisters (see p59)*, or join a Cape Malay cooking class.

10 Company's Garden
Established in 1652 as a vegetable garden to provide fresh produce to Dutch East India Company ships docking at Table Bay, the Company's Garden doubles as a botanical garden. At the heart of Museum Mile, this inner-city park, with a backdrop of Table Mountain, is a great place for a stroll *(see pp12–13)*.

Iziko Slave Lodge
HORSE-DRAWN CARRIAGE
St George's Cathedral
City Hall
The Company's Garden Restaurant
Iziko South African Museum
Buitenkant Street
Castle of Good Hope
The Company's Garden
District Six Museum
Mount Nelson Hotel

▶ MORNING

After breakfast, make your way to the **District Six Museum** *(see pp18–19)* and explore its stirring exhibits. Then walk a couple of blocks down Buitenkant Street to the **Castle of Good Hope** *(see pp20–21)*, leaving time to admire the **City Hall** *(see p21)*, where Mandela made his first public address after his release in 1990. At the castle, join one of the free guided tours that run daily at 11am. At noon, return to the main gate for the firing of the signal cannon. Either drop in at the castle's two museums or enjoy an early lunch at De Goewerneur. Afterwards, join the horse-drawn carriage tour (book ahead) of historic Cape Town – it departs at 12:45pm – and alight at the **Company's Garden** *(see pp12–13)*.

AFTERNOON

If you didn't have lunch at the castle, and the weather's nice enough to eat alfresco, **The Company's Garden Restaurant** *(see p12)*, opposite the aviary, has to be first choice. Then take a stroll around the gardens, followed by a visit to one of the museums lining them, such as the **Iziko South African Museum** and the **Iziko Slave Lodge** *(see p13)*. If it's a gloomy day, visit St George's Cathedral (see p13) or take the kids to a star show at the **Planetarium** *(see p13)* at the Iziko South African Museum. If you're feeling peckish, stroll to **Mount Nelson Hotel** *(see p114)* to sample its legendary tea buffet (2:30–5:30pm) before heading back to your hotel.

See map on pp66–7 ←

The Best of the Rest

1 St George's Mall
MAP Q4

Running through the heart of the historic city centre, this pedestrian mall is usually buzzing with street musicians and busy market stalls.

2 Iziko South African Museum

Mainly featuring natural history displays, the South African Museum also exhibits prehistoric rock art (see pp13 & 42).

3 South African Jewish Museum

MAP P6 ■ Hatfield St ■ 021 465 1546 ■ Open 10am–5pm Sun–Thu, 10am–2pm Fri ■ Adm ■ www.sajewish museum.co.za

Located in the country's oldest synagogue, this fascinating museum documents the history of South Africa's Jewish community.

4 Green Point Urban Park
MAP M1 ■ Fritz Sonnenberg Rd ■ Open 7am–7pm daily

Part of a much larger development that includes the 2010 World Cup stadium, the park is a great leisure space. Nearby is the red-and-white-striped Green Point Lighthouse.

5 Signal Hill and Lion's Head
MAP M3

The climb or drive up Signal Hill is highly rewarding. Be there at sunset for stunning views over the Atlantic.

6 Iziko Planetarium

The centrally located Planetarium has daily shows introducing the dazzling southern sky – worthwhile for those heading into the Karoo, with its clear and brilliant night sky (see p13).

White sands at a beach in Clifton

7 Clifton Beaches
MAP A2

The closest beaches to the city centre, the four picturesque, sheltered coves at Clifton are divided by giant boulders.

8 Springbok Experience Rugby Museum

MAP P1 ■ Portswood Rd, V&A Waterfront ■ 021 418 4741 ■ Open 9am–5pm Tue–Sun ■ Adm ■ www.sarugby.co.za

This museum documents the history of rugby from the 1860s, chiefly celebrating the "Springboks", South Africa's national team.

9 Church Square
MAP Q5

Flanked by grand old buildings on the west side stands the imposing Groote Kerk, South Africa's oldest church. A monument marks the fact that slaves were once traded here.

10 Iziko Maritime Centre

MAP P1 ■ Union-Castle House, Dock Rd, V&A Waterfront ■ 021 405 2880 ■ Open 9am–5pm daily ■ Adm ■ www.iziko.org.za

Tracing the history of shipping in Table Bay, exhibits at this museum include model boats and photographs from the mail-ship era.

Signal Hill and Lion's Head

Shops, Malls and Markets

1 V&A Waterfront
The Waterfront combines a wonderful harbourfront setting with a selection of shops and restaurants that is second to none (see pp14–15).

2 Pan African Market
MAP Q4 ▪ 76 Long St ▪ 021 426 4478
This is an excellent place to check out crafts from all over Africa. Along with a cheerful café, you'll also find a hairdresser and tailor here.

Mask, Pan African Market

3 Cape Quarter
MAP P3 ▪ 27 Somerset Rd ▪ 021 421 1111 ▪ www.cape quarter.co.za
Cape Quarter has a historic location in the trendy De Waterkant suburb and houses shops specializing in crafts and jewellery. It also has several restaurants and cafés.

4 Long Street
MAP P5
Those seeking a colourful shopping experience will enjoy Long Street's cult, craft and second-hand shops.

5 South African Market
MAP P4 ▪ 107 Bree Street ▪ 083 690 6476 ▪ www.ilovesam.co.za
South African designers come together to sell their work at this cavernous space on trendy Bree Street. It's a great place to pick up unique clothing, jewellery or quirky pieces of home decor.

6 The Neighbourgoods Market
MAP H1 ▪ 373 Albert Rd, Woodstock ▪ Open 9am–2pm Sat ▪ www. neighbourgoodsmarket.co.za
This trendy food market at the revived Old Biscuit Mill is the place to mingle with hip Capetonians on Saturdays.

7 Milnerton Flea Market
021 551 7879 ▪ Open Sat, Sun & some public holidays
This eclectic flea market is a great place to find some unusual items.

8 OZCF Market
MAP P1 ▪ Beach Road, Granger Bay ▪ Open 9am–2pm Sat
As well as fresh produce from the Oranjezicht City Farm (see p60), you can buy freshly baked bread, artisanal cheese and free-range meat.

9 The Woodstock Exchange
MAP H1 ▪ 66–68 Albert Road, Woodstock ▪ 021 486 5999 ▪ www.woodstockexchange.co.za
This uber-hip centre is home to young designers, artisans and other creatives. Pick up one-of-a-kind clothing or acquire a unique artwork.

Items at The Woodstock Exchange

10 Greenmarket Square
Situated on Greenmarket Square, Cape Town's oldest flea market has a definite buzz about it. A variety of African crafts can be found alongside ethnically inspired clothing and jewellery (see p67).

See map on pp66–7

Organized Activities and Day Tours

1 Cape Peninsula Day Tour

Organized tours to magnificent Cape Point also take in the Boulders Penguin Colony and include stops on the Atlantic Seaboard (see pp32–3).

Tourists at the Cape of Good Hope

2 Cape Town Carriage Company

021 704 6908 ▪ Departures 10:30am, 12:45pm & 2:45pm (booking required) ▪ www.ctcco.co.za

This horse-drawn carriage tours historic Cape Town, departing from the Castle of Good Hope and trotting along to the Company's Garden and surrounding museums.

3 City Sightseeing Bus

Cape Town open-top bus tours take in the city's main sights, while a separate route heads to Hout Bay and Constantia (see pp112–13).

4 Wine-Tasting Tour

The ideal way to enjoy wine-tasting is through the organized tours available out of Stellenbosch, Cape Town and Franschhoek.

5 District Six and Townships Tour

Typical tours start with a visit to the District Six Museum or Bo-Kaap, before moving on to the Langa and Khayelitsha townships. Lunch is at a local eatery or *shebeen* (bar) (see pp112–13).

6 Robben Island

Cape Town's most popular organized excursion is a guided tour of Robben Island via return boat trip from Nelson Mandela Gateway at the V&A Waterfront (see pp16–17).

7 Whale- and Dolphin-Watching Cruise

Best undertaken in calm weather, cetacean-viewing excursions into Table Bay – though not as certain to produce whales as Hermanus – can be organized through kiosks lining the V&A Waterfront (see pp14–15).

8 Table Bay Helicopter Trips

Several companies based at the V&A Waterfront offer thrilling helicopter trips with superb aerial views over Table Mountain and the city (see p52).

9 Inverdoorn Game Reserve

MAP V3 ▪ Off R46 ▪ 021 422 0013 ▪ www.inverdoorn.com

Set in the stunning Karoo, this reserve boasts abundant wildlife, including white rhinos (see p47).

Giraffes at Inverdoorn Game Reserve

10 Table Mountain Day Hike

Hike Table Mountain ▪ 021 422 0560 ▪ www.hiketablemountain.co.za

Experienced hikers will enjoy the hiking possibilities offered at Table Mountain. All hikes are best undertaken with a knowledgeable local guide to avoid being caught out by sudden weather changes.

Bars and Cafés

Sleek interior of the Bascule Whisky and Wine Bar

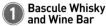

1 Bascule Whisky and Wine Bar

MAP Q2 ■ Cape Grace, West Quay Rd, V&A Waterfront ■ 021 410 7082

Enjoy South Africa's largest selection of whiskies at this waterfront bar. There's also a good wine list, beer on tap and whisky-tasting evenings.

2 The Taproom at Devil's Peak Brewing Company

H1 ■ 95 Durham Ave, Salt River ■ 021 200 5818

Grab a selection of this micro-brewery's excellent beers and watch the brewers at work.

3 The House of Machines

MAP P4 ■ 84 Shortmarket St ■ 021 426 1400

It's all bare brick walls and unpolished wood at this small bar known for its cocktails and craft beer. There are also regular live music nights.

4 Grand Café & Beach

MAP P1 ■ Haul Rd, Granger Bay ■ 021 425 0551

Enjoy a café-style dining experience on the deck or on the private beach with magnificent views of the ocean.

5 The Gin Bar

MAP P4 ■ 64a Wale St

This side-street bar serves only gin. Vie for a seat in the tiny courtyard and sip one of four signature cocktails showcasing gins from Cape Town's booming micro-distillery scene.

6 Sky Bar and Daddy Cool

MAP P4 ■ 38 Long St ■ 021 424 7247

The Sky Bar is on the rooftop terrace of the Grand Daddy Hotel, which offers Silver Bullet Airstream trailers for accommodation with a difference. Downstairs is the Daddy Cool Bar, where the decor is kitsch but trendy.

7 Beerhouse on Long Street

MAP P5 ■ 223 Long St ■ 021 424 3370

Enjoy Cape Town's biggest selection of local, international and craft beers in a pleasant, relaxing environment.

8 Neighbourhood Restaurant, Bar & Lounge

MAP P4 ■ 163 Long St ■ 021 424 7260

A gastro-pub with a games room and a balcony overlooking Long Street.

9 Truth Coffee

MAP Q5 ■ 36 Buitenkant St ■ 021 200 0440

Cape Town's coolest coffee shop is as much about its steampunk style as it is about the perfect cup of coffee.

10 Planet Bar

MAP P6 ■ 76 Orange St ■ 021 483 1000

A sophisticated crowd frequents this bar at the Mount Nelson Hotel for after-work drinks. Outdoor tables overlook manicured grounds.

See map on pp66–7

Music Venues and Nightclubs

Traditional musicians playing at Mama Africa

① Mama Africa
MAP P5 ■ 178 Long St
■ 021 426 1017 ■ www.mamaafrica
restaurant.co.za

Traditional music accompanies a pan-African menu and lively African decor at this legendary bar and restaurant.

② Shimmy Beach Club
MAP R1 ■ South Arm Rd,
V&A Waterfront ■ 021 200 7778
■ www.shimmybeachclub.com

This hip nightclub doubles as a fine dining destination in the daytime. It offers live music and great views of the Atlantic from its beach deck.

③ Coco
MAP P4 ■ 70 Loop St ■ 072
673 6869 ■ www.cococpt.co.za

Book ahead for this upmarket club. Music varies depending on the day – expect house, hip hop, R & B and trance.

④ DecoDance
MAP L3 ■ 120 Main Rd, Sea
Point ■ 021 434 3437

Cape Town's busiest nightclub plays rock and pop music from the 1960s to the 1990s. No entry for under-22s.

⑤ The Piano Bar
MAP P3 ■ 47 Napier St,
De Waterkant ■ 021 418 1096
■ www.thepianobar.co.za

Offering creative cocktails and tapas, this music revue bar has live entertainment and a wraparound terrace.

⑥ Dizzy's
MAP G1 ■ 41 The Drive,
Camps Bay ■ 021 438 2686
■ www.dizzys.co.za

There's always something going on here, including karaoke, beer-pong tournaments and live bands.

⑦ ThirtyOne Cape Town
MAP Q4 ■ 31st Floor, ABSA
Building, 2 Riebeek St ■ 021 421 0581
■ www.thirtyone.co.za

Admire panoramic views of Cape Town from this nightclub on the 31st floor. Open on Friday and Saturday, it attracts a well-dressed, older crowd.

⑧ Fiction
MAP P5 ■ 226 Long St
■ 021 422 0400

Great local DJs create a vibrant atmosphere with different music nights Tuesday to Saturday. There is a very small dance floor.

⑨ The Crypt Jazz Restaurant
MAP P4 ■ 1 Wale St ■ 079 683
4658 ■ www.thecryptjazz.com

Based in the Crypt of St George's Cathedral, this restaurant has live jazz and a varied dinner menu.

⑩ Crew Bar
MAP P3 ■ 30 Napier St,
Green Point ■ 073 204 3706

A vibrant gay bar offering top local music acts and stylish decor. It has a dance floor, VIP bar and verandahs.

See map on pp66–7

Theatre and Entertainment

1 Artscape Theatre Centre
MAP R4 ■ D F Malan St ■ 021 410 9800 ■ www.artscape.co.za
Cape Town's premier performing arts complex hosts ballet, opera and cabaret performances.

2 Labia Cinema
MAP P6 ■ 68 Orange St ■ 021 424 5927 ■ www.thelabia.co.za
This art cinema, named after its benefactor, Princess Labia, shows quality commercial movies and special-interest films.

3 Cape Town Comedy Club
MAP P2 ■ 3 The Pumphouse, V&A Waterfront ■ 021 418 8880 ■ www.capetowncomedy.com
Steaks, pizzas and burgers are on the menu, served with a side order of home-grown comedy. You often have to share a table, and you'll need to book in advance for special offers.

4 Stardust
MAP R5 ■ 118 Sir Lowry Rd, Woodstock ■ 021 462 7777 ■ www.stardustcapetown.com
Between courses of Mediterranean cuisine at this fun dinner-cabaret, the serving staff take to the stage to sing well-known covers.

5 City Hall
MAP Q5 ■ Darling St ■ 021 410 9809 ■ www.cpo.org.za
The impressive golden Italian Renaissance-style City Hall is the main concert venue for the Cape Philharmonic Orchestra.

6 Zip Zap Circus
MAP R4 ■ Jan Smuts St ■ 021 421 8622 ■ www.zip-zap.co.za
The city's non-profit circus school puts on shows, with proceeds given to social-outreach programmes.

7 Theatre on the Bay
MAP G1 ■ 1A Link St, Camps Bay ■ 021 438 3301 ■ www.pietertoerien.co.za
Stand-up comedy, musicals and conventional farces are the staples of this charming theatre.

8 Magnet Theatre
MAP H1 ■ Lower Main Rd, Observatory ■ 021 448 3436 ■ www.magnettheatre.co.za
As well as theatre and dance, this venue offers social-upliftment programs, and many performers are young students from the area.

9 Baxter Theatre
MAP H1 ■ Main Rd, Rondebosch ■ 021 685 7880 ■ www.baxter.co.za
The Baxter has long been at the cutting edge of local theatre. It shows both mainstream productions and more challenging works.

10 The Fugard Theatre
MAP Q5 ■ 7 Caledon St ■ 021 461 4554 ■ www.thefugard.com
Named after South Africa's most famous modern playwright, Athol Fugard, Cape Town's world-class theatre, bioscope and events complex is located within historic District Six.

Magnificent City Hall

Eateries at the V&A Waterfront

Sevruga's bright verandah

① Sevruga
MAP Q1 ▪ Shop 4, Quay 5 ▪ 021 421 5134 ▪ RRR

A large and varied menu of good-quality dishes and an extensive wine list of mainly local producers.

② Quay Four
MAP Q1 ▪ 4 West Quay Rd ▪ 021 419 2008 ▪ RR

Two dining choices are on offer here. The Tavern offers pub fare, wooden tables and benches at the water's edge, while Upstairs at Quay Four is a more elegant option.

③ Mondiall
MAP Q2 ▪ Alfred Mall ▪ 021 418 3003 ▪ RR

The lunch menu features upmarket bistro fare including a Wagyu cheeseburger. Popular for weekend brunch with good Table Mountain views.

④ Willoughby & Co
MAP Q1 ▪ 6130 & 6132 Victoria Wharf Centre ▪ 021 418 6115 ▪ RRR

Seafood is the speciality at this place, which is particularly noted for its sushi and the selection of wines by the glass.

⑤ Baia Seafood Restaurant
MAP Q1 ▪ 6262 Victoria Wharf Centre ▪ 021 421 0935 ▪ RRR

This bright restaurant serves top-notch seafood and meat dishes. These are best enjoyed from the balcony with its fine views of Table Mountain.

⑥ Den Anker Restaurant and Bar
MAP Q2 ▪ Pierhead ▪ 021 419 0249 ▪ RR

This restaurant has a great seafront location and a high-ceilinged interior. Beer, mussels and other traditional Belgian specialities are served.

⑦ Belthazar Restaurant and Wine Bar
MAP Q1 ▪ 163 Victoria Wharf Centre ▪ 021 421 3753 ▪ RRR

An award-winning steakhouse specializing in meat and poultry. It claims to have the world's longest by-the-glass wine list.

⑧ Panama Jacks
MAP H1 ▪ Quay 500, Cape Town Harbour ▪ 021 448 1080 ▪ RR

Venture into the working docks of Cape Town by taxi to find this old shack of a restaurant. Select lobster or abalone from seawater tanks.

⑨ Nobu
MAP P2 ▪ One&Only Hotel, Dock Rd ▪ 021 431 4511 ▪ RRR

Nobu offers a memorable culinary experience in an exclusive setting. Sample classic Japanese cuisine with a contemporary touch.

⑩ Harbour House
MAP P1 ▪ Quay 4, 280 Dock Rd ▪ 021 418 4744 ▪ RRR

Superlative seafood dominates the menu at this Cape Town favourite (with a branch in Kalk Bay). Be sure to try the catch of the day.

Alfresco dining at Harbour House

Restaurants

PRICE CATEGORIES

For a three-course meal for one, including half a bottle of wine, cover charge, taxes and extra charges.

R under R200 **RR** R200–300 **RRR** over R300

1 The Test Kitchen
MAP H1 ■ 375 Albert Rd, Woodstock ■ 021 447 2337 ■ RRR

An award-winning and world-renowned restaurant, Test Kitchen's dedicated executive chef Luke Dale-Roberts serves inventive global-style cuisine. Book months ahead.

2 Planet Restaurant
MAP P6 ■ 76 Orange St ■ 021 483 1000 ■ RRR

The Mount Nelson Hotel is one of Cape Town's "grande dames", and, while the stuffy colonialism is gone, a distinct air of elegance remains. A South African twist on international cuisine satisfies its five-star clientele.

3 Savoy Cabbage
MAP P4 ■ 101 Hout St ■ 021 424 2626 ■ RRR

Savoy Cabbage is one of Cape Town's hottest dining experiences. The creative menu changes daily and is accompanied by a carefully selected wine list (see p59).

4 Aubergine Restaurant
MAP P6 ■ 39 Barnet St, Gardens ■ 021 465 0000 ■ RRR

This restaurant serves seafood, meat and vegetarian dishes with African, European and Asian influences.

5 Bukhara
MAP P4 ■ 33 Church St ■ 021 424 0000 ■ RRR

Cape Town's top Indian restaurant has a fabulous vegetarian selection on its menu.

6 Beluga
MAP P3 ■ The Foundry, Prestwich St ■ 021 418 2948 ■ RRR

Tucked away in the office district of Green Point, Beluga offers Eastern-influenced grills, seafood and excellent-value sushi.

7 Chef's Warehouse
MAP P4 ■ 92 Bree Street ■ 021 422 0128 ■ RR

There are no reservations at this busy spot. Most people come for the ever-changing "tapas for two" option.

Tables at atmospheric Africa Café

8 Africa Café
MAP P4 ■ 108 Shortmarket St ■ 021 422 0221 ■ RRR

A nightly pan-African buffet makes this a great option for sampling the varied flavours of the continent.

9 Gold Restaurant
MAP P3 ■ 15 Bennett St ■ 021 421 4653 ■ RRR

Experience Gold's African 14-course tasting menu. In the evening there's traditional dancers, drumming, hand-washing and Mali puppets.

Cheese at Culture Club Cheese

10 Culture Club Cheese
MAP P5 ■ 215 Bree St ■ 021 422 3515 ■ R

Come here for breakfast or lunch. As the name implies, the speciality is cheese – try one of their many takes on a grilled cheese sandwich.

See map on p66–7

TOP 10 Southern Suburbs

Cape Town's most significant cluster of suburban attractions lies amidst the prestigious belt of leafy residential properties that stretches southward from the city centre, flanked to the west by Table Mountain and to the east by the incongruously poor Cape Flats. An area of interest for nature lovers, Kirstenbosch and Tokai offer scenic surroundings for a stroll. The estates along the Constantia Wine Route are as enjoyable as their more far-flung counterparts around Stellenbosch.

Rhodes Memorial

1 Rhodes Memorial
MAP H1 ▪ 021 687 0000
▪ Restaurant: open 9am–5pm daily
▪ www.rhodesmemorial.co.za

One-time prime minister of the Cape and founder of the Rhodesias (now Zimbabwe and Zambia) (see p41),

C J Rhodes has a memorial dedicated to him on a lookout point below Devil's Peak, which offers memorable views across the Cape Flats. Built in Neo-Classical style, the monument has Doric columns and stone lions modelled on Nelson's Column.

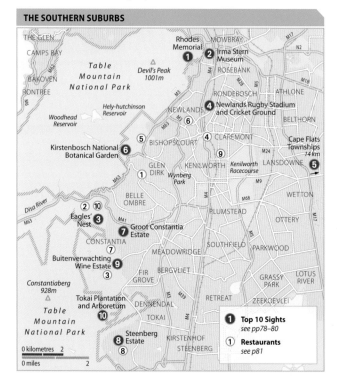

THE SOUTHERN SUBURBS

0 kilometres 2

0 miles 2

1 Top 10 Sights
see pp78–80

1 Restaurants
see p81

2 Irma Stern Museum

MAP H1 ▪ Cecil Rd, Rosebank
▪ 021 685 5686 ▪ Open 10am–5pm
Tue–Fri; 10am–2pm Sat ▪ Adm
▪ www.irmastern.co.za

This underrated museum opened in 1971 in the house where versatile artist Irma Stern lived till her death in 1966. Trained in Germany, Stern gained international acclaim for her impressionist portraits, but her idealized rendition of African subjects provoked controversy at home. As well as her paintings, the museum also houses Stern's collection of Africana, notably an early 20th-century Congolese stool.

3 Eagle's Nest

MAP H2 ▪ Old Constantia
Main Road, Constantia ▪ 021 794
4095 ▪ 10am–4:30pm daily ▪ Adm for
tasting ▪ www.eaglesnestwines.com

One of Constantia's lesser-known wineries, Eagle's Nest is a peaceful and picturesque spot for a tasting – the floral Viognier is one of their most celebrated wines. Dining options are simple, and in summer you can enjoy a picnic in the leafy grounds.

4 Newlands Rugby Stadium and Cricket Ground

MAP H2

Newlands hosted its first international rugby test match in 1891. A multipurpose venue with a crowd

Iconic sports venue Newlands

capacity of 51,900, it is home to one of South Africa's Super Rugby teams (see p54). Nearby, towering Table Mountain looms over the scenic Newlands Cricket Ground.

5 Cape Flats Townships

MAP C3, H1

Practically uninhabited until the 1940s, the sandy flats on the east of the peninsula were urbanized after the forced relocation of locals from whites only suburbs to townships such as Khayelitsha, Langa and Gugulethu. Despite upliftment, poverty is still high.

6 Kirstenbosch National Botanical Garden

This beautiful botanical garden extends up to the eastern slopes of Table Mountain. It has a rich selection of flora and birdlife typical to the Western Cape. The network of wide footpaths, some suitable for wheelchair users, leads visitors onwards and upwards to explore the *fynbos*-draped slopes of Table Mountain (see pp26–7).

Magnificent Kirstenbosch National Botanical Garden

Rolling vineyards of the historic Groot Constantia Wine Estate

⑦ Groot Constantia Wine Estate

South Africa's oldest wine estate is situated in the suburb of Constantia, below the eastern contours of Table Mountain. The opportunity to taste the award-winning wines alone justifies a visit, as does the stately Manor House *(see pp28–9)*.

⑧ Steenberg Estate

MAP H3 ▪ **Steenberg Rd, Tokai** ▪ **021 713 2211** ▪ **Tasting 10am–6pm daily; cellar tours: 11am & 3pm Mon– Fri** ▪ **www.steenbergfarm.com**

Located on the oldest farm in the Constantia Valley, and set below the eponymous "Stone Mountain", Steenberg was established in 1682 as Swaaneweide by Catharina Ras. Its award-winning wines are headed by a superb Sauvignon Blanc reserve and a red blend bearing Catharina's name. The estate has a champion-ship golf course attached *(see p54)*.

⑨ Buitenverwachting Wine Estate

MAP H3 ▪ **Klein Constantia Rd, Constantia** ▪ **021 794 5190** ▪ **Tasting 9am–5pm Mon–Fri, 10am–5pm Sat** ▪ **www.buitenverwachting.co.za**

Translated as "Beyond Expectations" – an allusion to the 100-tonne grape harvest reaped by Ryk Cloete in 1825 – this 18th-century Cape Dutch homestead is set at the foot of Constantia Mountain. Though the flagship wine is a Bordeaux-style blend (Christine), the estate also produces unblended reds and whites.

⑩ Tokai Plantation and Arboretum

MAP H3 ▪ **Tokai Rd** ▪ **021 712 7471** ▪ **Open Apr–Sep: 8am–5pm daily; Oct–Mar: 7am–6pm daily** ▪ **Adm** ▪ **www.sanparks.org**

Set in Table Mountain National Park, this pine-tree plantation encloses a Victorian arboretum and is popular with bird-watchers. Its winged residents include the forest buzzard and Verreaux's eagle. The Plantation is a managed forest, and areas may be closed for harvesting.

Tokai Plantation and Arboretum

Restaurants

1 Greenhouse
MAP H2 ▪ 93 Brommersvlei Rd, Constantia ▪ 021 795 6226 ▪ RRR

Gorgeous fusion cuisine is served at this stylish restaurant in The Cellars-Hohenort hotel (see p116).

2 Beau Constantia
MAP H2 ▪ Constantia Main Rd ▪ 021 794 8632 ▪ RR

Take in the stunning views and choose between sushi and platters of cheese, charcuterie and fresh bread to enjoy with your wine tasting.

3 Buitenverwachting Restaurant
MAP H2 ▪ Buitenverwachting, Klein Constantia Rd ▪ 021 794 3522 ▪ RRR

Set in a thatched Cape Dutch building, this restaurant combines continental and local influences. Also on the estate, Coffee BloC offers breakfasts and light lunches.

4 A Tavola
MAP H2 ▪ Wilderness Rd, Claremont ▪ 021 671 1763 ▪ RR

A rather humdrum location, but the authentic Italian food amply compensates. From a terrace table you can glimpse Table Mountain.

5 Moyo Kirstenbosch
In Kirstenbosch National Botanical Garden, Moyo's menu includes filled pancakes, sandwiches and picnic baskets (see pp26–7).

6 Myoga
MAP H2 ▪ Vineyard Hotel, 60 Colinton Rd, Newlands ▪ 021 657 4545 ▪ RRR

Lunch outdoors in the leafy gardens with Table Mountain etched against the skyline, or indoors in the Art Deco-inspired restaurant. The food is a fusion of eastern and western cuisine – try the seven-course tasting menu with wine pairings (see p116).

7 Jonkershuis Restaurant
MAP H2 ▪ Groot Constantia Wine Estate ▪ 021 794 6255 ▪ RR

This pleasant restaurant, set on the historic Groot Constantia Wine Estate, offers a hearty Cape Malay menu. Lunch is best enjoyed at outdoor tables under the giant oaks.

Chic setting at Bistro Sixteen82

8 Bistro Sixteen82
MAP H3 ▪ Steenberg Estate, Tokai ▪ 021 713 2211 ▪ RR

The bistro and tapas menu raises the standard of casual dining to an art form without the prices to match.

9 Banana Jam Café
MAP H2 ▪ 157 Second Ave, Kenilworth ▪ 021 674 0186 ▪ RR

This colourful restaurant serves good-value pizza and burgers, plus Caribbean dishes. There's a brewpub upstairs with 30 local beers on tap, and a vast collection of rums from the Caribbean islands.

10 La Colombe
MAP H2 ▪ Silvermist Wine Estate, Constantia ▪ 021 794 2390 ▪ RRR

Perched on the side of a mountain with views over the Constantia Valley, this relaxed yet ultra-elegant spot serves contemporary cuisine fusing local ingredients with French flair.

See map on p78

⏏🔟 The Cape Peninsula

The Cape Peninsula is a mountainous sliver of land that extends southward from Cape Town to Cape Point, and is flanked by the open Atlantic to the west and False Bay to the east. Two-thirds of the coastline along the north of the peninsula are studded with quaint villages, sandy beaches and pretty seaside resorts. In the south, the ragged mountain spine supports a cover of unspoilt *fynbos* interspersed with plantation forest. Most of the peninsula is protected within Table Mountain National Park (TMNP). Visitors could spend a lifetime exploring it, but highlights include the Cape of Good Hope, the penguin colony at Boulders Beach near Simon's Town, and lovely beaches at Muizenberg, Noordhoek and Fish Hoek.

Night heron in the Rondevlei Nature Reserve

THE CAPE PENINSULA

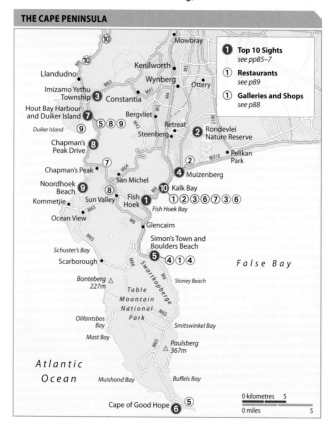

1 Top 10 Sights
see pp85–7

1 Restaurants
see p89

1 Galleries and Shops
see p88

The village of Fish Hoek and its magnificent beach

1 Fish Hoek
MAP H4

The quaint village of Fish Hoek lies at the mouth of the Silvermine River between Muizenberg and Simon's Town, and boasts one of the warmest and safest swimming beaches on the Peninsula. The clifftop Jager's Path offers good vantage points for whale watching. Overlooking the town is Peers Cave, one of the Cape's most important archaeological sites, which contains evidence of human occupation dating back 11,000 years.

2 Rondevlei Nature Reserve
MAP H3 ▪ Perth Rd, Rondevlei ▪ 021 706 2404 ▪ Open 7:30am–5pm daily; Dec–Feb: 7:30am–5pm Mon–Fri, 7:30am–7pm Sat & Sun ▪ Adm

A short drive north of Muizenberg, Cape Town's best bird sanctuary is home to 230 marine and freshwater species, which can be glimpsed from the short walking trail that connects its hides. Grebes, rails, herons and gulls are represented here. Hippos were introduced in 1982 to control the spread of surface vegetation.

3 Imizamo Yethu Township
MAP G2 ▪ City Sightseeing: 086 173 3287; tours 10:30am–4pm daily ▪ Adm ▪ www.citysightseeing.co.za

An isiXhosa phrase meaning "Our Efforts", this township was established on the outskirts of Hout Bay after the collapse of apartheid in the 1990s. It grew rapidly and is now a community of around 34,000 people living in rudimentary houses. One-hour guided walks of IY (the local name for the township) are offered by the City Sightseeing Bus.

4 Muizenberg
MAP H3

This resort town on False Bay was the location chosen a century ago by Witwatersrand gold magnates to build a row of seafront mansions. Historical sights include Het Posthuys, built as a tollhouse in 1742, battlements that are remnants of the 1795 Anglo-Dutch Battle of Muizenberg, the Edwardian railway station and Rhodes Cottage Museum, where C J Rhodes died in 1902. The wide, sheltered beach is a real haven for surfers and swimmers.

Rhodes Cottage Museum, Muizenberg

Penguin colony at Boulders Beach

5 Simon's Town and Boulders Beach

A naval base for over 200 years, the pleasantly time-warped Simon's Town is enhanced by the "Historic Mile", a row of Victorian façades lining St George's Street. The Victorian railway station is the southern terminus of one of the world's great suburban train rides, following the False Bay seafront to Muizenberg. The penguin colony south of town at Boulders Beach is the main attraction *(see pp30–31)*.

6 Cape of Good Hope

This reserve is the scenic highlight of the peninsula, dotted with stunning viewpoints such as Rooikrans, Gifkommetjie and Cape Point. It is a key stronghold for the Cape's unique *fynbos* habitat and for wildlife such as the eland and the endemic bontebok *(see pp32–3)*.

Cape of Good Hope's rugged point

7 Hout Bay Harbour and Duiker Island

MAP G3 ■ Hout Bay ■ Tours hourly

Hout Bay's busy little harbour is the launching point for boat trips to Duiker Island, a flat granite outcrop that lies about 6 km (4 miles) offshore. The island's rocky shores support 5,000–6,000 Cape fur seals. People are forbidden from landing on the island, but plenty of seals can be seen from the boats, which also have windows for underwater viewing. Various marine birds including black oystercatchers, African penguins and the breeding colonies of three different cormorant species may also be spotted here.

Vertiginous Chapman's Peak Drive

8 Chapman's Peak Drive

MAP G3 ■ Adm for vehicles
■ www.chapmanspeakdrive.co.za

Named after the peak that soars above it, Chapman's Peak Drive, constructed in 1915–22, is a stunning stretch of road. Set into an almost-vertical cliff face that connects Hout Bay to Noordhoek, the drive offers great viewing points and is now a toll road after years of repair work.

CAPE FLORAL KINGDOM

The smallest of the world's six floral kingdoms, the Cape consists of a unique floral community known as *fynbos* (fine bush), a reference to the narrow leaves of many plants. A UNESCO World Heritage Site and a biodiversity hotspot for its floral wealth, the Cape Peninsula supports almost 20 per cent of Africa's flora – home to an estimated 9,000 plant species.

 Noordhoek Beach
MAP G3

An expanse of bone-white sand running from the base of Chapman's Peak to Kommetjie, Noordhoek is the most beautiful beach on the Cape Peninsula. It is a lovely spot for walks and bird-watching; visitors may even catch a glimpse of the endangered black oystercatcher. Horse riding is also on offer here *(see p54)*.

 Kalk Bay
MAP H3

This artsy seaside suburb has plenty to keep its visitors occupied. The Olympia Café *(see p89)* is a favourite breakfast haunt, where you can fuel up for a day browsing the many galleries, boutiques and antiques shops lining Main Road *(see p88)*. Restaurants specializing in seafood line the waterfront, and you can wander the pier watching the busy fisherman bringing in their latest catch. Keep an eye out for the seals that climb up onto the harbour in search of fishy morsels, much to the fishmongers' dismay.

A FULL-DAY DRIVING TOUR TO CAPE POINT

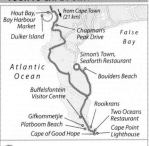

MORNING

After an early breakfast, head down to the Atlantic Seaboard via Camps Bay to **Hout Bay**. Once there, go on the 40-minute boat excursion to see the seals on **Duiker Island**, and, if it's the weekend, pop into **Bay Harbour Market** *(see p88)*. Then continue your journey with stops along **Chapman's Peak Drive** to enjoy the view, driving south to the **Cape of Good Hope** sector of **Table Mountain National Park** *(see p45)*. Stop at the **Buffelsfontein Visitor Centre** before you reach the Cape Point car park. If you're already peckish, enjoy a scenic lunch at the **Two Oceans Restaurant** *(see p89)* overlooking False Bay, or wait until after you've climbed the steep footpath (or caught the funicular) to **Cape Point Lighthouse** *(see p33)*.

AFTERNOON

Walk off the lunch following the footpath from the car park to the Cape of Good Hope Beach, or drive back along the main road through the reserve towards the entrance gate, diverting to the **Rooikrans**, **Gifkommetjie** or **Platboom Beach**. Leave by 3pm, following the road that hugs the False Bay coast towards **Simon's Town**. Stop occasionally to look out for whales. Before you reach Simon's Town, turn right for **Boulders Beach** to watch the squabbling penguins. Before driving back, enjoy a coffee at **Seaforth Restaurant** *(see p89)*, overlooking the harbour in Simon's Town.

See map on p84 ←

Galleries and Shops

1 Kalk Bay Gallery
MAP H3 ▪ 62 Main Rd, Kalk Bay ▪ 021 788 1674

This gallery specializes in fine art by local artists. You can have works shipped to anywhere in the world.

2 Artvark Gallery
MAP H3 ▪ 48 Main Rd, Kalk Bay ▪ 021 788 5584

A contemporary gallery showcasing South African art and crafts, plus custom and exclusive steelworks.

3 Kalk Bay Modern
MAP H3 ▪ 136 Main Rd, Kalk Bay ▪ 021 788 6571

Local modern art, textiles and crafts are featured in this gallery.

4 Quayside Centre
MAP H4 ▪ Simon's Town

A sophisticated complex below the Quayside Hotel (see p116), this centre has a range of curio shops, an art gallery and places to eat overlooking Simon's Town's harbour.

5 ...& Banana
MAP G2 ▪ 35 Main Rd, Hout Bay ▪ 021 790 0802

Find good-quality local wood items with a seaside theme and jewellery made by hand using organic materials, such as shells, beads and gemstones, at this original gift shop.

Quagga Rare Books & Art

6 Quagga Rare Books & Art
MAP H3 ▪ 86 Main Rd, Kalk Bay ▪ 021 788 2752

This highly regarded bookshop has numerous antiquarian titles.

7 Papagayo
MAP H3 ▪ 1 Belmont Rd, Kalk Bay ▪ 021 788 1923

Bargains can be found at this large warehouse piled high with colourful handicrafts, textiles, clothing and decor items.

8 Longbeach Mall
MAP G3 ▪ Cnr Buller Louw Dr & Sunnydale Rd, Noordhoek ▪ 021 785 5955

The southern peninsula's largest shopping centre contains more than 100 shops and leisure venues including supermarkets, a craft market, restaurants and cafés.

9 Bay Harbour Market
MAP G2 ▪ 31 Harbour Rd, Hout Bay ▪ 083 275 5586

Filled with craft stalls, quirky clothes and lots of good food, this is one of Cape Town's best markets.

10 Rose Korber Art
MAP G1 ▪ 48 Sedgemoor Rd, Camps Bay ▪ 021 433 0957

This renowned art dealer displays a collection of works by leading contemporary South African artists.

Shell accessories at ...& Banana

Restaurants

1 Lighthouse Café
MAP H4 ▪ 90 St Georges St, Simon's Town ▪ 021 786 9000 ▪ R

It doesn't boast the location that some Simon's Town restaurants have, but the friendly atmosphere and honest, affordable food more than make up for there being a road between you and the ocean.

2 Tiger's Milk
MAP H3 ▪ Beach Rd, Muizenberg ▪ 021 788 1860 ▪ RR

Grab a spot by the huge, ocean-facing windows and enjoy local craft beer with a pizza, burger or "bunny chow", a local speciality consisting of curry in a hollowed-out loaf of bread.

3 Harbour House
MAP H3 ▪ Kalk Bay Harbour ▪ 021 788 4136 ▪ RRR

This upstairs restaurant is as close to the ocean as you can get inside Kalk Bay Harbour, with huge glass windows looking out onto the ocean. It offers understated fine dining.

Harbour House's ocean view

4 Seaforth Restaurant
MAP H4 ▪ Seaforth Beach, Simon's Town ▪ 021 786 4810 ▪ RR

This seafood restaurant serves excellent pasta and pizza. Combine with a visit to the penguins (see p86).

5 Two Oceans Restaurant and Snack Bar
MAP H6 ▪ Cape Point ▪ 021 780 9200 ▪ Closed for dinner ▪ RRR

Famed for its fine Cape seafood and sublime sushi, this first-rate

> **PRICE CATEGORIES**
> For a three-course meal for one, including half a bottle of wine, cover charge, taxes and extra charges.
> ....
> R under R200 RR R200–300 RRR over R300

restaurant at Cape Point is also known for its truly staggering views across False Bay.

6 Olympia Café
MAP H3 ▪ 134 Main Rd, Kalk Bay ▪ 021 788 6396 ▪ RR

People queue here for the laid-back seaside atmosphere, excellent breakfasts and Mediterranean dishes.

7 The Foodbarn
MAP G3 ▪ Noordhoek Farm Village, Village Lane, Noordhoek ▪ 021 789 1390 ▪ RRR

Chef Franck Dangereux is a master of taste and flavour. The restaurant reflects French gastronomy, while the deli serves light meals and takeaway pies and quiches.

8 Kitima
MAP G2 ▪ 140 Main Rd, Hout Bay ▪ 021 790 8004 ▪ RR

In a historic Cape Dutch building, Kitima serves flavourful pan-Asian cuisine with an emphasis on Thai classics. The canapé menus offer dim sum, sushi and Asian tapas.

9 Dunes
MAP G2 ▪ 1 Beach Rd, Hout Bay ▪ 021 790 1876 ▪ RR

On the sands of Hout Bay beach, this bistro serves everything from tapas, salad and seafood to steaks and pizzas. It's good for families, and has a children's playground.

10 Azure Restaurant
MAP G2 ▪ Victoria Rd, Camps Bay ▪ 021 437 9029 ▪ RRR

Set in the prestigious Twelve Apostles Hotel (see p114), this gourmet restaurant combines Cape cuisine with international elements.

See map on p84 ←

TOP 10 The Winelands

The mountainous territory immediately inland of Cape Town, often referred to as the Boland (literally "Uplands"), is among the most beautiful parts of South Africa, and is dotted with lush, well-watered valleys amongst its rugged sandstone peaks. This region also forms the heart of the country's wine industry, and is home to around 300 wineries. The Winelands' historic towns include Stellenbosch, Franschhoek, Tulbagh and Paarl.

Climbing in the Jonkershoek

1 Jonkershoek Nature Reserve

MAP E3 ■ 021 866 1560 (Jonkershoek Valley) ■ Jonkershoek Valley and Assegaaibosch: open Apr–Oct: 8am–6pm daily; Nov–Mar: 8am–7pm daily ■ adm ■ www.capenature.co.za

This mountainous reserve on the outskirts of Stellenbosch is

THE WINELANDS

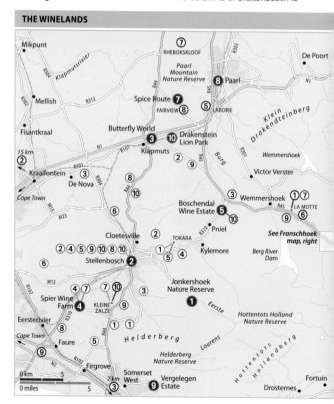

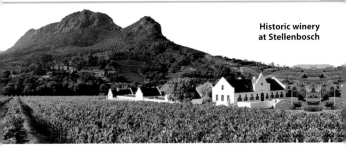

Historic winery at Stellenbosch

traversed by hiking trails, ranging from easy paths through the farmland of the Assegaaibosch sector to the demanding hikes to the upper slopes. The mountain scenery hosts more than 1,100 species of *fynbos* plants and a wide range of birds. The large mammal population includes leopards, baboons and klipspringers.

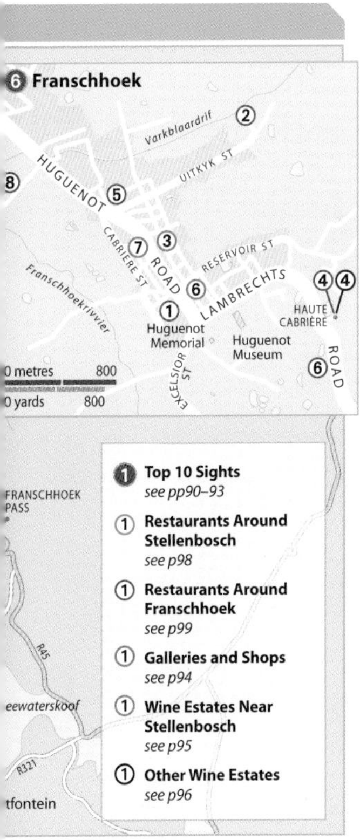
6 Franschhoek
Varkblaardrif
UITKYK ST
HUGUENOT
RESERVOIR ST
CABRIERE ST
ROAD
LAMBRECHTS
Franschhoekrivier
HAUTE CABRIÈRE
Huguenot Memorial
Huguenot Museum
EXCELSIOR ST
ROAD
0 metres 800
0 yards 800
FRANSCHHOEK PASS
R45
eewaterskoof
R321
tfontein
Top 10 Sights see pp90–93
Restaurants Around Stellenbosch see p98
Restaurants Around Franschhoek see p99
Galleries and Shops see p94
Wine Estates Near Stellenbosch see p95
Other Wine Estates see p96

2 Stellenbosch

The tourist capital of the Winelands lies amid mountainous surrounds on the banks of the Eerste River. Established just 27 years after Cape Town was settled, Stellenbosch is South Africa's second-oldest town and boasts the country's highest concentration of pre-20th-century Cape Dutch buildings. Despite its historic feel, Stellenbosch is anything but staid, thanks partly to the bustling student life associated with its university. The compact town centre is lively – and very safe – even after dark *(see pp34–5)*.

3 Butterfly World

MAP D1 ■ R44, Klapmuts ■ 021 875 5628 ■ Open 9am–5pm daily ■ Adm ■ www.butterflyworld.co.za

Butterfly World is South Africa's largest butterfly park and supports more than 20 indigenous free-flying species in an attractive, landscaped indoor garden. It is also home to small antelopes and iguanas, as well as tarantulas and other spiders in terrariums. There's a tea garden, a picnic area and a craft shop on site.

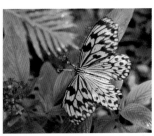

Idia butterfly at Butterfly World

CAPE DUTCH HOUSES

Cape Dutch architecture evolved in the 18th century, adapting European styles to suit African conditions. Its defining feature, derived from medieval houses in Amsterdam, is an ornate round gable above the entrance. Typical buildings, such as the manor at Vergelegen, have a thatched roof and a H-shaped floorplan.

 Spier Wine Farm

MAP D3 ▪ Off R310 en route Stellenbosch ▪ 021 809 1100 ▪ Tasting 9am–5pm Mon–Wed, 9am–6pm Thu–Sat, 11am–6pm Sun ▪ Adm ▪ www.spier.co.za

This beautiful estate is one of South Africa's oldest wine farms. The sophisticated wine-tasting venue, on the banks of the Spier Dam, pairs Spier signature wines with innovative food and also offers a children's grape juice tasting menu. The estate has a picnic hamper service, the Eight to Go Deli, a spa, a playground, a craft shop, Eagle Encounter shows, restaurants and the superb Spier Hotel (see p117), with its impressive and modern decor.

Boschendal Wine Estate

Boschendal Wine Estate

The pioneering Boschendal Estate was first planted with vines by Huguenot settler Jean de Long in 1685. Set in a green valley flanked by the Groot Drakenstein and Simonsberg Mountains, the estate is reached via a tree-lined drive. The Cape Dutch architecture here includes a manor house dating to 1812 and a cellar built in 1795. There's a restaurant and café, but, on fine days, the French-style "Le Pique-Nique" on the lawns is irresistible (see p36).

Franschhoek

MAP F2

Franschhoek is the self-styled culinary capital of South Africa. With a French influence that dates back to its settlement by Huguenot refugees in the late 17th century, its history is documented in the Huguenot Memorial Museum. Many wineries are to be found nearby, and stylish shops and world-class restaurants line the main street (see pp36–7).

Spice Route

MAP E1 ▪ Suid Agter Paarl Rd, Paarl ▪ 021 863 5200 ▪ Open 9am–5pm daily ▪ www.spiceroute.co.za

At this artisans' village, everything is brewed, distilled, cured, baked or fermented on site. Join a chocolate tasting, learn how charcuterie is produced, taste outstanding wines, visit the microbrewery, and finish your day with food ranging from wood-fired pizza to spice-rubbed steak.

Paarl

MAP E1 ▪ 021 872 4842 ▪ www.paarl online.com

Hemmed in by Paarl Mountain to the west and the Berg River to the east, the largest town in the Winelands is a bit scruffy com-pared to Stellenbosch. Paarl Mountain, a granite outcrop in a nature reserve, and the Afrikaans Language Monument are worth a visit, and the Laborie Wine Estate is charming.

The Afrikaans Language Monument, Paarl

Garden walkway at Vergelegen

9 Vergelegen Estate

MAP E4 ▪ L-ourensford Rd, Somerset West ▪ 021 847 2100 ▪ Open 9am–5pm (last entry 4pm) daily ▪ Adm ▪ www.vergelegen.co.za

Translated as "lying afar", this historic property on the slopes of the Helderberg started life as a remote outpost of the Cape Colony in 1685. Fifteen years later, it became the private estate of Willem van der Stel, who established the elegant manor house and octagonal garden, and planted the gnarled camphor trees at its entrance. This is one of South Africa's premier estates for its magnificent grounds and range of wines, and it is well worth making the journey here.

10 Drakenstein Lion Park

MAP E1 ▪ Old Paarl Rd (R101), Klapmuts ▪ 021 863 3290 ▪ Open 9:30am–5pm daily ▪ Adm ▪ www. lionrescue.org.za

This park, founded in 1998, provides lifelong sanctuary to captive-born big cats that have been abused or suffered distress and would not be able, because of their upbringing, to fend for themselves in the wild. More than 30 of these magnificent animals live freely and safely in over 20 ha (50 acres) of natural habitat. Chimp Haven is also a popular draw, but the highlight of a visit is to sleep overnight in the tented camp set within the lions' territory.

THE "FOUR PASSES" DAY CIRCUIT

▶ MORNING

The circuit around the **Hottentots Holland Mountains** encompasses some of the Winelands' finest scenery, architecture and wine estates. Starting in **Stellenbosch** *(see pp34–5)*, drive south along the R44 towards **Somerset West**. Follow the signs to the **Vergelegen Estate** on the Helderberg slopes. Once here, explore the historic buildings and pause for a coffee or a wine tasting. From Somerset West, follow the N2 east via **Sir Lowry's Pass**, then turn left onto the R321, passing through **Grabouw** and over **Viljoen Pass** before descending into the **Riviersonderend** "River Without End" Valley to **Theewaterskloof Dam**. Turn left onto the R45, which traverses the **Franschhoek Pass**, offering wonderful views over the town whose name it bears.

AFTERNOON

In **Franschhoek**, cruise the main road to choose a lunch spot from one of the many excellent dining establishments. Then pop into the **Huguenot Memorial and Museum** *(see p37)* or browse the shops along the main street. Continue west along the R45 and stop at **L'Ormarins Wine Estate** to visit the **Franschhoek Motor Museum** *(see p36)*. Outside Franschhoek, branch left onto the R310 to reach Stellenbosch via the **Helshoogte Pass**. Stop en route at the **Boschendal Wine Estate**, the town of **Pniel** and **Hillcrest Berries Farm**. End your day with a drink at the Tokara estate's restaurant *(see p95)*.

See map on pp90–91

Galleries and Shops

1 Root 44 Market
MAP D3 ▪ Audacia Wines, R44/Annandale Rd, Stellenbosch ▪ 021 881 3052

This lively market is one of the Winelands' finest. Open every weekend, it's not just a place to shop for crafts and organic food – you can have lunch, taste beer and wine, and listen to live music while the kids enjoy the playground.

2 Oom Samie Se Winkel
MAP D2 ▪ 84 Dorp St, Stellenbosch ▪ 021 887 0797

Stellenbosch's most famous *winkel* (shop) is over 100 years old and retains a Victorian appearance. It features an eclectic range of affordable local craftwork and genuine Africana.

3 The Ceramics Gallery
MAP F2 ▪ 24 Dirkie Uys St, Franschhoek ▪ 021 876 4304

View beautiful, utilitarian pottery by David Walters and even watch him working at the wheel.

Root 44 Market

Karoo Classics' elegant leather goods

4 Karoo Classics
MAP D2 ▪ Cnr Bird & Church sts, Stellenbosch ▪ 021 886 7596

Handcrafted accessories made of the softest mohair, local ostrich leather and other natural, regional materials are the speciality at this shop in Stellenbosch's town centre.

5 Local Works Arts & Crafts
MAP D2 ▪ 10 Drostdy St, Stellenbosch ▪ 021 887 0875

This impressive little shop has a collection of handpicked pieces that highlight the diversity of African art and culture.

6 Is Art Franschhoek
MAP F2 ▪ 11 Huguenot Rd, Franschhoek ▪ 021 876 2071

Named after owner Ilse Schermers Griesel, this vibrant gallery showcases contemporary South African art as well as local antiques and collectables.

7 Huguenot Fine Chocolates
MAP F2 ▪ 62 Huguenot Rd, Franschhoek ▪ 021 876 4096

Delicious chocolates created by two local Belgian-trained chocolatiers are sold at this popular boutique.

8 Vineyard Connection
MAP D2 ▪ Delvera Farm, Cnr R44 & Muldersvlei Rd, Stellenbosch ▪ 021 884 4360

This shop, located between Paarl and Stellenbosch, stocks the Cape's finest wines and can ship overseas.

9 Sasol Art Museum
MAP D2 ▪ 52 Ryneveld St, Stellenbosch ▪ 021 808 3691 ▪ Open 10am–4:30pm Mon, 9am–4pm Tue–Sat

This tiered, Neo-Classical building displays the university's collection of 19th- and 20th-century art, and an anthropological collection of traditional African crafts and household objects.

10 Rupert Museum
A superb collection of contemporary South African art amassed by Dr Anton Rupert is housed in this gallery *(see p35)*.

→ *See map on pp90–91*

Wine Estates Near Stellenbosch

1 Rust en Vrede
MAP D3 ▪ Annandale Rd, Stellenbosch ▪ 021 881 3881 ▪ Tasting 9am–5pm Mon–Sat ▪ www.rustenvrede.com

This was the first wine estate to specialize in premium red wines only. It also has a great restaurant.

2 Rustenberg Wines
MAP E2 ▪ Lily Rd, Ida's Valley ▪ 021 809 1200 ▪ Tasting 9am–4:30pm Mon–Fri, 10am–4pm Sat, 10am–3pm Sun ▪ www.rustenberg.co.za

This 300-year-old farm is known for its crisp Chardonnays.

3 Villiera
MAP D3 ▪ R304 ▪ 021 865 2002 ▪ Open 9am–5pm Mon–Fri, 9am–3pm Sat ▪ www.villiera.com

Before you try a tasting of MCC (Méthode Cap Classique), you can join a guided game drive to see zebra, giraffe and a host of antelope.

4 Delaire Graff
A "vineyard in the sky" on the crest of Helshoogte Pass, Delaire Graff makes good reds, and its grounds are perfect for picnics (see p36).

5 Tokara
Located on Helshoogte Pass, Tokara has a scenically positioned restaurant. As well as its acclaimed wines, it is renowned for its superb olive oil (see p36).

Vineyard views for diners at Tokara

6 Simonsig
MAP D2 ▪ Kromm Rhee Rd ▪ 021 888 4900 ▪ Tasting 8:30am–4:30pm Mon–Fri, 8:30am–3:30pm Sat, 11am–2:30pm Sun; tours 11am Mon–Sat ▪ www.simonsig.co.za

South Africa's first producer of MCC offers an excellent, free cellar tour explaining the process. Tours end with a demonstration of the *sabrage* – opening a bottle with a sword.

7 Spier Wine Farm
This estate has mid-priced, very quaffable wines and lots of family-oriented activities (see p92).

8 Meerlust
MAP D3 ▪ R310 ▪ 021 843 3587 ▪ Tasting 9am–5pm Mon–Fri, 10am–2pm Sat ▪ www.meerlust.co.za

At Meerlust, the cellar is stocked with the iconic claret-style Rubicon blend.

9 Blaauwklippen
MAP D3 ▪ R44 ▪ 021 880 0133 ▪ Open 10am–6pm Mon–Sat, 10am–5pm Sun ▪ www.blaauwklippen.com

This estate offers a quaility Zinfandel and is home to a historic manor house, a bistro and a Sunday craft market. There are pony rides for kids.

10 Kanonkop
MAP D2 ▪ R44 ▪ 021 884 4656 ▪ Tasting 9am–5pm Mon–Fri, 9am–2pm Sat ▪ www.kanonkop.co.za

As well as several award-winning blends, Kanonkop also produces one of South Africa's finest Pinotages.

Other Wine Estates

La Motte's tasting room

1 ## La Motte
MAP F2 ▪ R45 Main Rd, Franschhoek ▪ 021 876 8000 ▪ Tasting 9am–5pm Mon–Sat ▪ www.la-motte.com

Award-winning wines in a lovely spot in the Franschhoek Valley (see p37).

2 ## Durbanville Hills
MAP C2 ▪ M13, Tygervalley Rd ▪ 021 558 1300 ▪ Tasting 10am–4:45pm Mon–Fri, 10am–3:15pm Sat, 11am–3:15pm Sun ▪ www.durban villehills.co.za

Visit the Durbanville Hills estate for some excellent plummy Merlots.

3 ## Waterkloof
MAP D4 ▪ Sir Lowry's Pass Rd, Somerset West ▪ 021 858 1292 ▪ Tasting 10am–5pm Mon–Sat, 11am–5pm Sun ▪ www.waterkloof wines.co.za

Set in a space-age glass box perched on a slope, Waterkloof's tasting lounge and restaurant have incredible views of False Bay, the Hottentots Holland and Helderberg mountains. The estate is known for its elegant wines.

4 ## Haute Cabrière
MAP F2 ▪ Franschhoek Pass Rd ▪ 021 876 2630 ▪ Tasting 9am–5pm Mon–Fri, 10am–4pm Sat, 11am–4pm Sun ▪ www.cabriere.co.za

Haute Cabrière produces world-class sparkling wines. The corks are removed with a sword.

5 ## Laborie
MAP E1 ▪ Taillefer St, Paarl ▪ 021 807 3390 ▪ Tasting 9am–5pm Mon–Sat, 11am–5pm Sun ▪ www.laboriewines.co.za

Located in the heart of Paarl since 1698, Laborie is famous for its Shiraz, Merlot and Méthode Cap Classique.

6 ## Leopard's Leap
MAP F2 ▪ R45 Main Rd, Franschhoek ▪ 021 876 8002 ▪ Tasting 9am–5pm Tue–Sat, 11am–5pm Sun ▪ www.leopardsleap.co.za

This modern tasting room, with elements of wood, glass and chrome, has a colourful range of wine cocktails.

7 ## Rhebokskloof
MAP E1 ▪ Windmeul, Agter Paarl ▪ 021 869 8386 ▪ Tasting 9am–5pm Mon–Fri, 10am–3pm Sat & Sun ▪ www.rhebokskloof.co.za

Encircled by mountains, this estate offers leisure and adventure activities.

8 ## Fairview
MAP E1 ▪ Suid-Agter Paarl Rd ▪ 021 863 2450 ▪ Tasting 9am–5pm daily ▪ www.fairview.co.za

A popular estate, Fairview produces fine wines and has a superb deli that serves handcrafted goat's cheese.

9 ## Vergenoegd
MAP D3 ▪ Baden Powell Dr, R310 ▪ 021 843 3248 ▪ Tasting 9am–5pm Mon–Fri, 10am–4pm Sat & Sun ▪ www.vergenoegd.co.za

This estate features a wine-blending experience, cellar tours and picnics. Children will enjoy the large flock of Indian runner ducks.

10 ## Kleine Zalze
MAP D3 ▪ R44, Stellenbosch ▪ 021 880 0717 ▪ Tasting 9am–6pm Mon–Sat, 11am–6pm Sun ▪ www.kleinezalze.co.za

Best known for its restaurant Terroir (see p98), this estate also has a golf course and charming guest rooms (see p117).

Iconic Wines

1 Kanonkop Paul Sauer
This is one of South Africa's most celebrated Bordeaux blends, led always by Cabernet Sauvignon. It has a restrained style, and is medium-bodied with a very well-judged level of oak.

2 Boekenhoutskloof Syrah
Marc Kent's reputation in the wine industry was established in 1997 when he produced this wine with his first harvest. Now an industry benchmark, it leans towards Old World styling, but the taste is proudly individual.

3 Beyerskloof Pinotage Reserve
Made from South Africa's "own" grape, this wine was created in the early 1920s by crossing Pinot Noir with Cinsaut (known as Hermitage). Beyers Truter's name is synonymous with Pinotage, and this is a particularly good one.

4 Hamilton Russell Vineyards Pinot Noir
This Hemel-en-Aarde Valley property pioneered Pinot Noir in South Africa in the 1970s. Juxtaposing power and restraint, the wine's typical raspberry/cherry core is always well wrapped in assertive yet controlled tannins.

5 Beaumont Hope Marguerite Chenin Blanc
Chenin Blanc is the South African wine industry's workhorse, and finds its way into sparkling wines, dry table wines, sweet wines and brandy. This wine is smooth and fruitful but serious, with reined-in oaking.

6 Ken Forrester The FMC Chenin Blanc
As extravagant and outgoing a Chenin Blanc as Ken Forrester himself, this wine is individualistic, complex and sweet when it first hits the palate but with enough tang to finish long and dry.

7 Graham Beck Cuvée Clive
Produced only when the vintage is particularly fine, Cuvée Clive is the most prestigious Cap Classique méthode champenoise wine from an estate famed for its bubbly.

8 Nederburg Edelkeur Noble Late Harvest
The first Cape Noble Late Harvest (always made from Chenin Blanc), this wine exudes melon and apricot flavours, while limey acidity seams the sweetness and converts it into delicious nectar.

9 Meerlust Rubicon
A true icon, established in 1693 and owned by the Myburgh family since 1756, this is one of South Africa's first and best-known Bordeaux blends, with several prestigious awards to its name.

Tasting bar at Meerlust Estate

10 Cape Point Isliedh
With vineyards located right in the teeth of the Cape's notorious wind, where only white grapes can reach full ripeness, this is a white Bordeaux blend in which Sauvignon Blanc's stone fruit and herbs are enhanced by Sémillon and a touch of new oak. It benefits from long cellaring.

See map on pp90–91

Restaurants Around Stellenbosch

1 Tokara Delicatessen
MAP E2 ▪ Helshoogte Pass
▪ 021 808 5950 ▪ Closed dinner ▪ R–RR
Created with Tokara's wide range of artisanal produce, this delicatessen offers healthy, good-value fare, and is great for weekend brunch. For fine dining try Tokara Restaurant.

Delicatessen at Tokara

2 Glen Carlou
MAP E2 ▪ R45/Simondium Rd, Klapmuts ▪ 021 875 5528 ▪ RRR
Based in the tasting room of the Glen Carlou Winery, this restaurant delivers perfectly presented plates of food with equally delicious views.

3 Makaron
MAP D3 ▪ 26–32 Houtkapper St, Stellenbosch ▪ 021 880 1549 ▪ Closed lunch ▪ RRR
Located at Majeka House, a boutique hotel and spa, Makaron is renowned for serving excellent cuisine that showcases local specialities.

4 Eight
MAP D3 ▪ Spier Wine Farm, R310, Stellenbosch ▪ 021 809 1100 ▪ RRR
Boasting an open-plan kitchen and garden tables, Eight offers an inventive fine food menu using organic produce grown locally. For lighter meals visit Eight To Go Deli or the Spier Hotel restaurant.

5 96 Winery Road
MAP D3 ▪ Winery Rd (off R44), Somerset West ▪ 021 842 2020 ▪ RR
This country-style place has a changing menu of seasonal dishes. It also has a private cellar packed full of vintage Cape reds.

6 Jordan Restaurant
MAP D3 ▪ Jordan Wine Estate, Stellenbosch Kloof Rd (off M12) ▪ 021 881 3612 ▪ RRR
The flavours of the locally sourced food at Jordan are intense, as are the fabulous vineyard views (see p59).

7 Terroir
MAP D3 ▪ Kleine Zalze Wine Estate, R44, Stellenbosch ▪ 021 880 8167 ▪ RRR
Terroir's changing Provençal-style chalkboard menu combines French and local influences (see p58).

8 Helena's
MAP D2 ▪ 33 Church St, Stellenbosch ▪ 021 883 3132 ▪ RRR
Set in the historic Coopmanhuijs Boutique Hotel (see pp116–17), Helena's serves delicious dishes using local ingredients.

9 Babel at Babylonstoren
MAP E2 ▪ Babylonstoren, Klapmuts-Simondium Rd, Klapmuts ▪ 021 863 3852 ▪ RRR
A simple menu reflects the colours and tastes of the season. Produce is gathered daily from the seasonal gardens.

Dish at Babel at Babylonstoren

10 Restaurant Jardine
MAP D2 ▪ 1 Andringa St, Stellenbosch ▪ 021 886 5020 ▪ RRR
A small but superb restaurant. The menu changes regularly, but the food is consistently excellent.

Restaurants Around Franschhoek

PRICE CATEGORIES
For a three-course meal for one, including half a bottle of wine, cover charge, taxes and extra charges.

R under R200 RR R200–300 RRR over R300

1 The Tasting Room at Le Quartier Français

MAP F2 ▪ 16 Huguenot Rd, Franschhoek ▪ 021 876 2151 ▪ Closed lunch ▪ RRR

A Franschhoek institution since the 1990s, the Tasting Room offers imaginative five- or eight-course menus (see p58).

2 Racine

MAP F2 ▪ Uitkyk St, Franschhoek ▪ 021 876 2393 ▪ RRR

Located on the Chamonix wine estate and run by celebrity chef Reuben Riffel, this restaurant has an innovative brasserie-style menu with African, Asian and European influences.

3 Fyndraai

MAP E2 ▪ Solms-Delta Wine Estate, off R45, Groot Drakenstein ▪ 021 874 3937 ▪ Closed dinner ▪ RRR

Well known for its modern take on traditional Cape cuisine, the menu here explores the culinary heritage of the area.

4 Haute Cabrière Restaurant & Terrace

MAP F2 ▪ Franschhoek Pass Rd, Franschhoek ▪ 021 876 3688 ▪ RRR

Offering stunning views from a 17th-century wine estate (see p96), this restaurant serves French and South African contemporary dishes.

5 Ryan's Kitchen

MAP F2 ▪ 1 Place Vendome, Huguenot Rd ▪ 021 876 4598 ▪ RRR

This restaurant's menu changes fortnightly. Expect local produce such as ostrich steak, Karoo lamb or Cape crayfish and salmon.

6 La Petite Ferme

MAP F2 ▪ Franschhoek Pass Rd, Franschhoek ▪ 021 876 3016 ▪ RRR

A glass veranda offers views over the Franschhoek Valley, and the global menu does the location full justice.

7 Pierneef à la Motte

MAP F2 ▪ R45 Main Rd, Franschhoek ▪ 021 876 8800 ▪ RRR

The name and wines are inspired by La Motte's gallery of Pierneef artworks, and the fare is a modern take on historic Cape Winelands cuisine (see p96).

8 Grande Provence Restaurant

MAP F2 ▪ Main Rd, Franschhoek ▪ 021 876 8600 ▪ RRR

This upmarket restaurant in the estate of the same name serves an à-la-carte menu, plus a six-course wine pairing.

Elegant interior of Grande Provence

9 Bread & Wine

MAP F2 ▪ Môreson Wine Farm, Happy Valley Rd, Franschhoek ▪ 021 876 3692 ▪ Lunch only ▪ R

This family-oriented lunch venue on the Môreson Estate serves tasty, inventive country cuisine.

10 The Werf Restaurant

MAP E2 ▪ Pniel Rd, Groot Drakenstein ▪ 021 870 4206 ▪ RRR

The Werf is the flagship fine-dining restaurant on the beautiful Boschendal Wine Estate (see p36), located in the Manor House cellar.

See map on p90–91

TOP 10 Beyond the Winelands

Assuming you can drag yourself away from its estimable charms, Cape Town provides a great base for exploring the rest of the Western Cape, a province notable for its consistently scenic coastline, *fynbos*-swathed mountains and ever-expanding winemaking industry. Highlights east of Cape Town include the peerless land-based whale watching in Walker Bay and the underrated De Hoop Nature Reserve – not to mention Agulhas, the most southerly tip of Africa – while the west coast up towards Lamberts Bay combines ruggedly beautiful seaside scenery with some of the world's most spectacular floral displays.

Young zebra at De Hoop

BEYOND THE WINELANDS

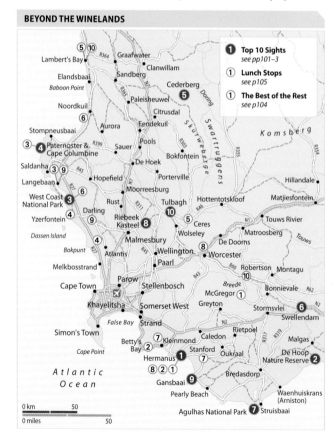

1 Top 10 Sights
see pp101–3

1 Lunch Stops
see p105

1 The Best of the Rest
see p104

1 Hermanus

MAP U5 ▪ Tourist information:
028 312 2629 ▪ www.hermanus
tourism.info

Southeast of Cape Town, the quaint small town of Hermanus is perched on sheer cliffs that hem in Walker Bay. Its attractions include the montane *fynbos* of Fernkloof Nature Reserve. But above all, Hermanus is the world's best place for land-based whale viewing from June to November. The movements of south-ern right whales, which regularly breach in the waters below town, are tracked by a "whale crier".

2 De Hoop Nature Reserve

MAP W5 ▪ 028 542 1114/5
▪ Open 7am–6pm daily ▪ Adm
▪ www.capenature.co.za

To the east of Agulhas, this is South Africa's largest surviving coastal *fynbos* habitat. It is a breeding ground for the endemic bontebok and Cape mountain zebra. The coastline of tall sand dunes and sheer cliffs can be explored on short walking and mountain biking trails, or along a five-day hiking trail named after the whales that breach offshore between June and November.

3 West Coast National Park

MAP S3 ▪ 022 772 2144/5 ▪ Main park: open Apr–Aug: 7am–6pm daily; Sep–Mar: 7am–7pm daily ▪ Adm ▪ Postberg Flower Reserve: open Aug & Sep: 9am–5pm daily ▪ Adm ▪ www.sanparks.co.za

Extending around the sparkling salt waters of the Langebaan Lagoon, this pristine coastline lies just an hour's drive north of Cape Town. Famous for the wild flowers in the Postberg sector, the park is also worth visiting for its variety of fauna, including eland, rock hyrax and many wetland bird species. Offshore islands support breeding colonies of ten different marine bird species *(see p45)*. The recreational zone of the lagoon is popular with watersports fans.

Gannets in West Coast National Park

4 Paternoster and Cape Columbine

MAP S2

The coastal village of Paternoster, located on Cape Columbine to the north of Cape Town, is renowned for its traditional white fishermen's cottages and superb crayfish. The adjacent Columbine Nature Reserve protects a lovely stretch of coast that bursts into spectacular bloom from August to October and offers excellent kayaking spots through the year.

Wild flowers, West Coast National Park

Prehistoric rock art on sandstone formations in the Cederberg

(5) Cederberg

MAP U2 ▪ 021 483 0190
▪ www.capenature.co.za

The Cederberg Wilderness (provincial reserve) and the Cederberg Conservancy (private farmland) form the heart of Cederberg. The area is revered for its stunning sandstone formations, its profusion of prehistoric rock art and its rich endemic flora and fauna. It is best explored over several days, but the conservancy also offers day hikes in montane and karoo territory, with private camps providing access to rock-art sites and views.

Old Drostdy interior, Swellendam

(6) Swellendam

MAP W5 ▪ Tourist Information: 028 514 2770; www.swellendam tourism.co.za

Founded in 1745 at the Cape Colony's remote eastern frontier, this small town has an old-world atmosphere reinforced by Cape Dutch buildings such as the Old Drostdy (Magistrate's Seat), which was built in 1747 and is now a local history museum. Beyond town lies the *renosterveld* (heath-like

land) of Bontebok National Park, established in 1931 to protect the 30 last remaining wild bontebok, whose population now numbers over 200.

(7) Agulhas National Park

MAP V6 ▪ 028 435 6078 ▪ Park: open 7:30am–6pm daily ▪ Lighthouse: open 9am–5pm daily ▪ Adm for lighthouse ▪ www.sanparks.co.za

The southernmost tip of Africa and the meeting point of the Atlantic and Indian Oceans, Agulhas, named by Portuguese navigators, means "needles", an allusion to the jagged offshore rocks that have caused around 250 shipwrecks. The park is home to South Africa's oldest lighthouse (built in 1849), and its rocky beaches have a stark charm.

(8) Riebeek Kasteel

MAP U3 ▪ Tourist information: 022 448 1545; www.riebeekvalley.info

Sitting in the Swartland region north of Cape Town, arty Riebeek Kasteel is a favourite weekend spot for Capetonians. Best known for its olives (an annual festival honouring

WHALES AND DOLPHINS

A remarkable 42 species of whales and dolphins have been recorded in South African waters. The Western Cape is the prime whale-spotting destination, thanks to the southern right whales that migrate to sheltered coves such as Walker and False bays. Bottle-nosed dolphins are regulars here too, pirouetting as they follow in a boat's wake.

the olive is held here each May), Riebeek Kasteel also has a growing number of wineries producing some superb reds. In the historic town centre you'll find all sorts of foodie delights – small restaurants, a coffee roaster, two microbreweries and a chocolatier among them. Neighbouring Riebeek West hosts a Saturday morning produce market.

9 Gansbaai

MAP U6 ■ Tourist information: 028 384 1439; www.gansbaaiinfo.com

This fishing village, named after the geese that once nested here, is known for the sharks and whales that live offshore. Shark safaris focus mostly on Dyer Island, which supports black oystercatchers, African penguins and the Cape fur seal colony. Nearby, the 2,000-year-old potshards unearthed at Klipgat Cave are among the oldest discovered in South Africa.

Fur seals at play in Gansbaai

10 Tulbagh

MAP U3 ■ Tourist information: 023 230 1375 ■ www.tulbaghtourism. co.za

The town of Tulbagh, below the Groot Winterhoek Mountains, was founded in 1700. While relatively remote from Cape Town, it makes a charming getaway. Boasting more than 30 Cape Dutch buildings, the centre exudes period character. The *fynbos*-draped mountains form an imposing backdrop, and offer good walking, horse-riding and bird-watching. The area supports over 20 wine estates.

OVERNIGHT TOUR TO HERMANUS

▶ DAY 1

Follow the N2 south-east from Cape Town for 45 minutes, turning right onto the R44 at Strand. **Hermanus** *(see p101)* is 75 km (47 miles) from Strand, so you could make it in an hour, but you'll want to stop to admire the glorious views from Clarence Drive across False Bay. **Harold Porter Botanical Garden** *(see p104)* in Betty's Bay is a great place to relax in a *fynbos* habitat. In Hermanus, check into a hotel and then lunch at the **Burgundy Restaurant** or grab a bite at beachfront **Dutchies** *(see p105)*. In the afternoon, follow the Cliff Path west out of town, or stroll around town keeping an eye out for whales. In calm weather, head to **Onrus Beach**. End with dinner at the **Burgundy** or **The Marine Hermanus** *(see p119)*.

▶ DAY 2

After an early breakfast, drive to **Gansbaai** for a cruise to **Dyer Island** to spot whales, dolphins and the fearsome great white shark. Alternatively, take a 2-hour boat-based whale cruise, or stay back and explore the town's boutiques. On the return trip to Gansbaai, stop off at **Marianas** *(see p105)* in Stanford for lunch, then head on towards the N2 and enjoy the splendid mountain views on the Houw Hoek and Sir Lowry's passes to **Somerset West**. If time permits, take a detour to the historic **Vergelegen Estate** *(see p93)*, located in the scenic Helderberg Mountains, and finish your day with a tasting.

See map on p100

The Best of the Rest

1 McGregor
MAP V4 ▪ www.tourism
mcgregor.co.za

Hidden away in the Langebergs, McGregor offers wine and olive tastings and mountain hikes.

2 Harold Porter National Botanical Garden
MAP E6 ▪ Betty's Bay ▪ 028 272 9311 ▪ Open daily ▪ Adm ▪ www.sanbi.org

This garden is dedicated to *fynbos* coastal flora, and is renowned for its waterfalls and amber pools.

3 Langebaan
MAP S3 ▪ www.langebaan-info.co.za

With ocean and lagoon to choose from, Langebaan is a very popular water-sports destination.

4 !Khwa ttu
MAP S3 ▪ R27, Yzerfontein ▪ 022 492 2998 ▪ Tours 10am & 2pm ▪ Adm ▪ www.khwattu.org

!Khwa ttu explores the fascinating history and culture of South Africa's indigenous people, the San.

5 Lambert's Bay
MAP T1 ▪ www.lamberts bay.co.za

Discover Bird Island's huge colony of Cape gannets plus Heaviside's dolphins and other cetaceans via boat trips.

6 Rocherpan Nature Reserve
MAP S2 ▪ 079 203 1092 ▪ Open 8am–5pm daily ▪ Adm ▪ www.capenature.co.za

The bird species in this seasonal wetland include the great white pelican and the great crested grebe.

Verdant Kogelberg Biosphere Reserve

7 Kogelberg Biosphere Reserve
MAP D5 ▪ 021 271 5138 ▪ Open 7:30am–4pm daily ▪ Adm ▪ www.capenature.co.za

A protected *fynbos* habitat that is great for hiking, biking and kayaking.

8 Karoo Desert National Botanical Garden
MAP U4 ▪ Roux Rd, Worcester ▪ 023 347 0785 ▪ Open 7am–7pm daily ▪ Adm ▪ www.sanbi.org

A largely uncultivated garden, known for its amazing displays of arid and semi-arid southern African plants.

9 Darling
MAP T3 ▪ www.darling tourism.co.za

This quaint town is known for its arts and craft shops, wild flowers, tea rooms, wine and cabaret.

10 Robertson
MAP V4 ▪ www.robertson tourism.co.za

Robertson lies along the Breede River wine route, where the estates offer better value than those around Stellenbosch and Franschhoek.

Vineyards around Robertson

Lunch Stops

> **PRICE CATEGORIES**
> For a three-course meal for one, including half a bottle of wine, cover charge, taxes and extra charges.
> ....
> **R** under R200 **RR** R200–300 **RRR** over R300

1 Origins at the Marine
MAP U5 ▪ Marine Dr, Hermanus ▪ 028 313 1000 ▪ RRR

This restaurant, in the five-star Marine Hermanus, is excellent for a light seafood lunch or a three-course dinner paired with wines. Enjoy a pre-meal cocktail in The Sun Lounge for views of the legendary whales breaching in the Walker Bay waters.

2 Dutchies
MAP U5 ▪ Grotto Beach, Hermanus ▪ 028 314 1392 ▪ RR

The cosmopolitan food served at Dutchies is enhanced by the attractive beachfront location. It's a great spot for watching whales.

3 Noisy Oyster
MAP S2 ▪ 62 St Augustine Rd, Paternoster ▪ 022 752 2196 ▪ RR

As the name suggests, seafood is the main focus of the menu here. Diners rave about West Coast oysters and mussels and the seafood *laksa*, a Malaysian-style spicy soup.

4 Hilda's Kitchen
MAP T3 ▪ R27, Darling ▪ 022 492 2825 ▪ Closed dinner ▪ RR

Based within the Groote Post winery, Hilda's specializes in tasty, honest country cooking. The menu changes on a daily basis, but a good range of meat, fish and pasta dishes can usually be expected.

5 Tolhuis Bistro
MAP U3 ▪ R43, Mitchell's Pass, Ceres ▪ 023 312 1211 ▪ Closed dinner ▪ R

Named after a former toll house (now a national monument) at Mitchell's Pass, this place serves great steaks and light lunches.

6 Geelbek Restaurant
MAP S3 ▪ West Coast National Park ▪ 022 772 2134 ▪ Closed dinner ▪ RR

Set in a Cape Dutch house, Geelbek specializes in South African fare.

7 Marianas
MAP U5 ▪ 12 Du Toit St, Stanford ▪ 028 341 0272 ▪ Open lunch Thu–Sun ▪ No credit cards ▪ RR

Mariana puts her passion into the food – using produce from her herb and vegetable garden – and husband Peter explains each delicious dish.

Characterful, elegant Burgundy

8 Burgundy Restaurant
MAP U5 ▪ Marine Dr, Hermanus ▪ 028 312 2800 ▪ RR

This sea view restaurant has an excellent Mediterranean-style menu. Now a heritage site, it's set in one of the oldest buildings in Hermanus.

9 Die Strandloper
MAP S3 ▪ Langebaan Lagoon ▪ 022 772 2490 ▪ No credit cards ▪ RRR

This place serves a tasty barbecued fish buffet. As this is weather dependent, booking is essential.

10 Muisbosskerm Restaurant
MAP S1 ▪ R365, 4 km (2 miles) south of Lambert's Bay ▪ 027 432 1017 ▪ RR

Linger over the buffet of Cape seafood dishes at this open-air restaurant on the beachfront.

See map on p100

Streetsmart

Brightly painted traditional houses
in the Bo-Kaap district of Cape Town

Getting To and Around Cape Town and the Winelands

Arriving by Air

The main gateway for international flights to South Africa is **OR Tambo International Airport** in Johannesburg. It is connected to Cape Town by numerous domestic flights. A few operators also fly directly to Cape Town from Europe or the Middle East, including **British Airways**, **Emirates** and **KLM**.

The **Cape Town International Airport** flanks the N2 highway 20 km (12 miles) east of the city centre. Regular flights connect Cape Town to Johannesburg and Durban, with less frequent services to Port Elizabeth, Bloemfontein and other South African cities. Fares with **South African Airways** tend to be pricier so seek out the budget operators **Mango**, **Kulula** and **Safair**.

The cheapest way to get from the airport to the city is on the MyCiTi bus, which leaves every 30 minutes and takes 25–30 minutes to get to the city centre. Registered taxi operators and shuttle services have stands in the airport.

Arriving by Train

It's unlikely that you'll arrive in Cape Town by train, as passenger services are infrequent. **Shosholoza Meyl** is the main operator, with routes to Johannesburg and East London. There are also two luxurious and expensive options – the **Blue Train**, which travels between Cape Town and Pretoria, and **Rovos Rail**, which travels to Pretoria and on to Victoria Falls.

Arriving by Sea

Cape Town is a port of call for cruise ships heading between the Indian Ocean Islands and Europe. The ships dock at the Cape Town Cruise Terminal at Duncan Dock in the **Port of Cape Town**, which is a 10-minute drive from the city centre and within walking distance of the V&A Waterfront.

Arriving by Road

Intercape, **Greyhound** and **Translux** buses connect Cape Town to major cities and popular tourist towns. **Adderley Street Bus Station** is the main terminal, and is located next to the train station.

Car-rental rates start at R170 per day and generally include 200 km (124 miles) free usage, though some offer unlimited mileage. Most major international players are represented. International operators such as **Avis** and **Hertz** are costlier than local companies such as **Around About Cars** and **Tempest**, though the best deals are usually found through consolidators such as **Argus Car Hire**.

Paid street parking is ample in the city centre at reasonable rates. Outside the city centre, you won't find a meter but you will often find a car guard.

These self-employed people will help direct you into a space and generally keep an eye on your car in return for small change – R2–5 is fine.

Speed limits are usually 120 kmph (75 mph) on major highways, and speed cameras are common. Look out for rapid drops in the speed limit. If you're ever stopped by police, never pay a fine at the side of the road – always insist on a ticket and pay the fine at a post office later on.

Getting Around by Bus

MyCiTi buses operate around town, to and from the airport, to the Table View area and along the Atlantic Seaboard to Hout Bay. To travel on the MyCiTi buses, you need to purchase a prepaid card. This can then be topped up at certain stores, some ATMs and at the major bus terminals. If you want to use the airport bus but won't be taking public transport afterwards, there is a single trip card available for R8.

Older **Golden Arrow** buses also operate around town and the suburbs, but they're not as comprehensive or user-friendly. Cash is accepted on board.

Getting Around by Train

The most useful train route is **Metrorail**'s Southern Route, which runs to Simon's Town and includes a very scenic stretch from Kalk Bay onwards. There's also a regular service to Stellenbosch. Buy a ticket before boarding and keep an eye on the stations you pass – there are no announcements or route maps on board. Trains are fine during the day, but avoid empty carriages and travelling after dark.

Minibus Taxis

Shared combi taxis are ubiquitous and the main form of public transport for most Capetonians. They can be hailed and are cheap, but you'll often wait a while for the seats to fill up. Still, they offer a snapshot of local life and are fine for short trips. Pay the driver's assistant once you have boarded – fares start at R8 for a short journey.

Taxis

Taxis in the city are good value at around R10/km. It's best to book ahead with a reputable operator such as **Excite**, **Rikki's** or **Intercab** rather than hailing on the street. The private taxi app **Uber** operates in Cape Town, the airport and some locations in the Winelands such as Stellenbosch.

On Foot

Most major attractions in central Cape Town are within walking distance of each other. Take advice from trusted locals about where not to go after dark.

Getting Around by Bicycle

Cape Town's cycle lanes are growing in number. **Bicycle Cape Town** has information on routes, laws and bike rental. **Up Cycles** rents out bicycles in the city centre, Sea Point Promenade, Camps Bay and the V&A Waterfront.

DIRECTORY

ARRIVING BY AIR

British Airways
🌐 britishairways.com

Cape Town International Airport
MAP C3
▪ Matroosfontein, Cape Town
📞 +27 (021) 937 1200
🌐 airports.co.za

Emirates
🌐 emirates.com

KLM
🌐 klm.com

Kulula
🌐 kulula.com

Mango
🌐 flymango.com

OR Tambo International Airport
Kempton Park, Gauteng
📞 +27 11 921 6262
🌐 airports.co.za

Safair
🌐 flysafair.co.za

South African Airways
🌐 flysaa.com

ARRIVING BY TRAIN

Blue Train
🌐 bluetrain.co.za

Rovos Rail
🌐 rovos.com

Shosholoza Meyl
🌐 shosholozameyl.co.za

ARRIVING BY SEA

Port of Cape Town
🌐 transnetnationalports authority.net

ARRIVING BY ROAD

Adderley Street Bus Station
MAP Q4 ▪ Adderley Street

Argus Car Hire
🌐 arguscarhire.com

Around About Cars
🌐 aroundaboutcars.com

Avis
🌐 avis.co.za

Greyhound
🌐 greyhound.co.za

Hertz
🌐 hertz.co.za

Intercape
🌐 intercape.co.za

Tempest
🌐 tempestcarhire.co.za

Translux
🌐 translux.co.za

GETTING AROUND BY BUS

Golden Arrow
🌐 gabs.co.za

MyCiTi
🌐 myciti.org.za

GETTING AROUND BY TRAIN

Metrorail
🌐 getgometro.com

TAXIS

Excite Taxis
📞 021 448 4444

Intercab
📞 021 447 7799

Rikki's Taxis
📞 0861 745 547

Uber
🌐 uber.com

GETTING AROUND BY BICYCLE

Bicycle Cape Town
🌐 bicyclecapetown.org

Up Cycles
🌐 upcycles.co.za

Practical Information

Passports and Visas

All travellers to South Africa need a valid passport. Visas are not required by nationals of EU countries, the US, Canada, Australia and New Zealand, who are given a free three-month visitor's permit on arrival. Citizens of most other countries will need a visa, and should consult the **Department of Home Affairs (DHA)** website for details of how to apply.

Anti-trafficking regulations require that travellers under the age of 18 must travel with an unabridged copy of their birth certificate stating the names of both mother and father. Check the DHA website for the latest regulations.

The **UK**, **US**, **Canada** and other countries have consular represen- tation in the region.

Customs Regulations

No duty is charged on items that are imported temporarily for personal use, and duty-free restrictions are standard. Non-residents can claim a VAT refund on leaving the country if the items they purchased can be inspected, so ask for a tax invoice when you buy expensive items.

Travel Safety Advice

Visitors can get up-to-date travel safety information from the **US Department of State**, from the **Australian**

Department of Foreign Affairs and Trade, and from the **UK Foreign and Commonwealth Office**.

Travel Insurance

Travel insurance is highly recommended; there is no public health service, which means that any medical bills of uninsured travellers will have to be paid by them at the time of treatment.

Health

Vaccinations advised for most tropical countries aren't really applicable to the Cape Town area, although you should get polio or tetanus boosters, if these have expired. Anyone travelling to Cape Town via a yellow fever area might be asked to show a vaccination certificate at immigration.

The standard of private healthcare is high, and it is relatively cheap compared to the US or Europe.

The Cape Town area has several excellent private hospitals including branches of **Mediclinic** and **Netcare**. **Groote Schuur** is a superb public hospital with an emergency department.

Most pharmacies keep standard business hours, but there are late-night and even 24-hour ones. The **Lite-Kem Pharmacy** is open until 11pm daily.

The rate of HIV infection in South Africa is very high, so take precautions. Condoms are readily available, with free dis-pensers in many toilets.

Personal Security

Although South Africa has a reputation when it comes to crime, it's fairly rare for a tourist to encounter anything other than the usual petty crime associated with larger cities. Take sensible precautions when walking around – don't flash your cash or valuables, lock away jewellery, passports and other valuables, avoid deserted parts of town and be particularly vigilant after dark. Avoid the city's townships after dark unless you're on an organised tour, and be sure that your ride home is in a registered taxi.

There have been some attacks on hikers walking the many footpaths of Table Mountain. Never hike alone and always tell someone which route you'll be taking.

Carjackings are incredibly rare in Cape Town but do be vigilant when waiting at red lights, particularly at night.

Two scams have been associated with ATMs. One involves a "helpful" local making off with your card; the other entails causing your card to get stuck mid-transaction. You are most vulnerable outside of banking hours and in remote locations. Never reveal your PIN to a stranger and ensure that nobody sees you type it in.

Tourists have been known to get mugged. If you are confronted by a robber with a weapon, hand over your belongings immediately and call the police afterwards.

Emergency Services

In an emergency, there are two central phone numbers for **Ambulance/Fire**, and for **Police**. There is also a seperate **emergency number from a mobile (cell) phone**.

Currency and Banking

South Africa's currency is the rand, locally denoted by the letter R, and internationally by ZAR, divided into 100 cents. Bank notes are in denominations of R10, R20, R50, R100 and R200. Coins come in denominations of 10c, 20c, 50c, R1, R2, R5.

Most banks are open 9am–3:30pm Monday-Friday. City banks are open 8:30–11:30am on Saturday.

Most banks have foreign exchange facilities, and private bureaux de change (locally known as forex bureaux) are also found in malls and airports, typically keeping longer hours than banks. All foreign exchange transactions are documented, and you must show your passport.

International credit and debit cards are accepted almost everywhere. You will be asked for "cheque" or "savings" when paying – this is only relevant to South African account holders, but say "cheque" to move things along.

Telephone and Internet

Cape Town has a 021 prefix, and the international code for South Africa is +27. Calls out of South Africa are prefixed by 00. Mobile (cell) phones are in wide use, and numbers start with 06, 07 or 08. If you are set up for international roaming, you can use your GSM phone in South Africa. A cheaper alternative is to buy a local SIM card (they usually cost less than R1). You need to "RICA" (register) your SIM before using it. To do this, you'll need a passport and proof of your address in South Africa in the form of a reservation confirmation, which can be supplied by your hotel or other accommodation.

Most hotels also offer internet facilities, but check to make sure you won't be charged. Free Wi-Fi is widespread, and you'll find it at many bars, restaurants, cafes, hotels, guesthouses and hostels. You need to sign up to get free Wi-Fi at airports.

Postal Services

International post in and out of South Africa is slow but reliable – airmail to Europe typically takes at least a week and to North America at least two. A faster service is offered by a private chain called **PostNet**, found in most large malls. Use an international courier for items of any value.

DIRECTORY

Newspapers, TV and Radio

Several English-language newspapers are available in Cape Town, notably the *Cape Argus*, *Cape Times*, *Sunday Times* and the *Mail & Guardian*.

The state broadcaster **SABC**'s three channels offer coverage in all 11 of the country's official languages, while **eTV** broadcasts international programmes. Many hotels and bars have satellite TV (DSTV) showing movies, TV series, sports and news.

SAFM is a national radio station focusing on news and current affairs. **Cape Talk** is the main local station.

Opening Hours

Post offices and government offices are open 8:30am to 4:30pm Monday to Friday. Post offices are also open 8:30 to 11:30am on Saturdays. Timings for sights do vary, so always check ahead.

Time Difference

South Africa is always 2 hours ahead of Greenwich Mean Time, and 6 hours ahead of the US Eastern Standard Summer Time.

Electrical Appliances

The South African plug has three round pins, though most hotel and guesthouse rooms also have sockets (or adaptors) for the twin-pronged plugs used in continental Europe. For appliances with any other plug, bring adaptors. The electricity supply is 220-230v/50Hz.

Weather

The warm summer months of October to March are peak tourist season. Winter has periods of beautiful, mild weather interspersed with days of cold, rain and wind. Late August–September is the best time to visit; it's not too crowded, the weather is good, and the spring wild flowers are on display.

Disabled Travellers

Facilities for disabled travellers in South Africa continue to improve, and most hotels, shopping malls and tourist sights have wheelchair access. Some public transport is accessible to wheelchairs, including MyCiTi buses and the City Sightseeing Bus.

If you rent a car, ask for a parking disc that allows for parking concessions. Some car-hire companies have vehicles with hand controls for drivers with disabilities.

Several tour operators specialize in itineraries for disabled travellers. **Flamingo Tours** and **Endeavour Safaris** both cater to most disabilities. A recommended operator on a national level is **Rolling South Africa**.

Sources of Information

The main **Cape Town Tourism** office is in the city centre and it offers general information on the city and Western Cape province. There are also offices at popular tourist spots and at the airport. **Franschhoek**, **Stellenbosch**, and the Winelands all have their own tourism websites.

Cape Town also has a host of blogs and lifestyle apps and magazines. **Zomato** is a nationwide restaurant-rating website and app. **EatOut** is great for anything food-related. **Mother City Living** focuses on markets and environmentally friendly happenings. **Cape Town Magazine** and What's on in Cape Town are also great for finding out about local events.

Trips and Tours

There is a range of companies offering tours or excursions in Cape Town and the Winelands.

City Sightseeing offers guided tours, including hop-on, hop-off bus trips, free walking tours, boat trips, helicopter flights, sidecar adventures and township tours. **Nielsen Tours** also offers free walking tours of the city centre or, for a more challenging hike, join **Table Mountain Walks** to explore Cape Town's most famous landmark. There are some really interesting themed tours of the city – **Coffee Beans Routes** offers art, fashion, beer and jazz trips among others, while **Andulela** is known for cooking tours.

There is no public transport to the Cape of Good Hope, so, if you don't plan to hire a car, a peninsula tour, such as **Cape Point Route**, is a good option. **Awol Tours** specializes in cycle tours, including day visits to the townships, the peninsula and the Winelands. If you visit the townships, it's best to go with a guided tour company, such as **Uthando**, which supports community development projects with the proceeds from tours.

Shopping

Cape Town has a number of large malls. Canal Walk in Century City is the biggest, while the Victoria Wharf Shopping Centre *[see p15]* is the most popular with tourists. For African curios, visit Greenmarket Square *[see p67]*, the Pan African Market on Long Street *[see p71]* or The Watershed at the V&A Waterfront *[see p15]*. Kalk Bay, Bree Street and Woodstock are known for their galleries, antiques and quirky boutiques.

Where to Eat

Cape Town has a lively dining scene and offers everything from cheap take aways to some of the world's best restaurants. Traditional Cape Malay food is difficult to find – try the family-run eateries in Bo-Kaap *(see p70)*.

Seafood along the peninsula is excellent, and South Africans are also enthusiastic meat-eaters, so you can expect great steaks and game meat. The best places for restaurants are on Bree, Kloof and Long streets *(see p77)*, Woodstock and the V&A Waterfront *(see p76)*.

Waiters and bar staff tend to depend on tips, which should be around the 10–15 per cent mark.

Where to Stay

Accommodation ranges from backpacker dorms to family-friendly budget hotels and five-star resorts. Self-catering accommodation is easy to find. Local booking sites include **WhereToStay** and **SafariNow**. Airbnb is also very popular in Cape Town. **Booking.com** has some good deals.

Prices vary hugely, from hostel en-suite doubles at around R600 a night to luxury suites that cost over R10,000. At peak times (Christmas and Easter) prices can skyrocket, and rooms need to be booked up months in advance. The best bargains can be found during the winter months (May–August).

DIRECTORY

NEWSPAPERS, TV AND RADIO

Cape Argus and Cape Times
w iol.co.za

Cape Talk
567 mw
w capetalk.co.za

eTV
w etv.co.za

Mail & Guardian
w mg.co.za

SABC
w sabc.co.za

SAFM
104–107 FM
w safm.co.za

Sunday Times
w timeslive.co.za

DISABLED TRAVELLERS

Endeavour Safaris
w endeavour-safaris.com

Flamingo Tours
w flamingotours.co.za

Rolling South Africa
w rollingsa.co.za

SOURCES OF INFORMATION

Cape Town Magazine
w capetownmagazine.com

Cape Town Tourism
MAP P4 ◼ Cnr Burg & Castle sts
w capetown.travel

EatOut
w eatout.co.za

Franschhoek
w franschhoek.org.za

Mother City Living
w mothercityliving.com

Stellenbosch
w stellenbosch.travel

What's on in Cape Town
w whatsonincapetown.com

Winelands
w winelands.co.za

Zomato
w zomato.com

TRIPS AND TOURS

Andulela
w andulela.com

Awol Tours
w awoltours.co.za

Cape Point Route
w capepointroute.co.za

City Sightseeing
w citysightseeing.co.za

Coffee Beans Routes
w coffeebeansroutes.com

Nielsen Tours
w nielsentours.co.za

Table Mountain Walks
w tablemountainwalks.co.za

Uthando
w uthandosa.org

WHERE TO STAY

Airbnb
w airbnb.com

Booking.com
w booking.com

SafariNow
w safarinow.com

WhereToStay
w wheretostay.co.za

Places to Stay

PRICE CATEGORIES
For a standard, double room per night (with breakfast if included), taxes and extra charges.

R under R1500   RR R1500–2500   RRR over R2500

Upmarket Hotels

Camps Bay Retreat
MAP G1 ▪ 7 Chilworth Rd, Camps Bay ▪ 021 437 8300 ▪ www.camps bayretreat.com ▪ RRR
Tucked away in a private nature reserve a few streets back from the ocean, this historic property has rooms in the main house or in a separate building reached by a rope bridge across a ravine. Children are welcomed, but the spa and rambling gardens also make it a peaceful spot for honeymooners.

Cape Grace
MAP Q2 ▪ West Quay Rd, V&A Waterfront ▪ 021 410 7100 ▪ www.cape grace.com ▪ RRR
The aptly named Cape Grace hotel offers stylish accommodation, a mind-boggling array of services, tasty Cape fusion cuisine and informal but attentive staff. Some rooms have private balconies.

Cape Heritage Hotel
MAP P4 ▪ 90 Bree St ▪ 021 424 4646 ▪ www. capeheritage.co.za ▪ RRR
This historic hotel has 17 individually decorated rooms with antique features such as 19th-century wood floors and high-beamed ceilings. South Africa's oldest vineyard is located in the courtyard.

The Cape Milner
MAP N5 ▪ 2a Milner Rd, Tamboerskloof ▪ 021 426 1101 ▪ www.capemilner. com ▪ RRR
A chic city hotel with 57 rooms decorated with flair in a refreshingly minimalist style. Services include a cocktail and tapas lounge, swimming pool and gym.

Mount Nelson Hotel
MAP P6 ▪ 76 Orange St, Gardens ▪ 021 483 1000 ▪ www.belmond.com ▪ RRR
With its iconic Victorian exteriors, elegant rooms, a fine-dining restaurant and grand views, the "Nellie" is undoubtedly the city's most prestigious hotel. The afternoon teas served with obsequious gravity on the patio are highly recommended.

One&Only Cape Town
MAP P2 ▪ Dock Rd, V&A Waterfront ▪ 021 431 5888 ▪ www.oneandonly resorts.com ▪ RRR
An urban resort with contemporary African flair, set in the heart of the trendy V&A Waterfront. It has 131 rooms and suites, 40 of them on an island in the marina.

The Twelve Apostles Hotel & Spa
MAP G2 ▪ Victoria Rd, Camps Bay ▪ 021 437 9255 ▪ www.12apostles hotel.com ▪ RRR
Located on the edge of the Atlantic Ocean and at the foot of the Twelve Apostles formation, this five-star boutique hotel has 70 exceptional rooms, superb service, a private cinema and an excellent spa. It also offers guided walks and picnics in the surrounding *fynbos*.

Victoria & Alfred Hotel
MAP P2 ▪ Pierhead, V&A Waterfront ▪ 021 419 6677 ▪ www.new markhotels.com ▪ RRR
Located in a converted Victorian warehouse, this hotel rises from the heart of the V&A Waterfront, ensuring that all the airy rooms have good views. Loft suites come with a heavier price tag than standard rooms.

Waterfront Village
MAP Q2 ▪ 4 West Quay Rd, V&A Waterfront ▪ 021 421 5040 ▪ www. waterfrontvillage.com ▪ RRR
A five-star apartment-and-suite complex that offers luxury self-catering accommodation, sleeping from two to six people. The many amenities, including five swimming pools, make it suitable for couples and families.

Westin Cape Town
MAP Q3 ▪ 1 Lower Long St ▪ 021 412 9999 ▪ www.westincapetown. com ▪ RRR
Geared towards business travellers, this hotel towers over the Cape Town International Convention Centre (CTICC). It has a rather characterless feel, but there's no quibbling with the five-star facilities.

Mid-Range Hotels

Cape Standard

MAP M2 ∎ 3 Romney Rd, Green Point ∎ 021 430 3060 ∎ www.cape standard.co.za ∎ RR

Small and reasonably priced, this hotel combines sleek modern European minimalism with subtle African touches to create a light, spacious feel. It's is within striking distance of the city centre.

Derwent House

MAP N6 ∎ 14 Derwent Rd, Tamboerskloof ∎ 021 422 2763 ∎ www. derwenthouse.co.za ∎ RR

This boutique hotel, set in the heart of the City Bowl, has rooms with views of Table Mountain. The stylish decor is complemented by excellent facilities, including a large deck, solar-heated pool and hot tub.

Four Rosmead

MAP N7 ∎ 4 Rosmead Ave, Oranjezicht ∎ 021 480 3810 ∎ www. fourrosmead.com ∎ RR

Built in 1903, this boutique guesthouse is set in a classified monument that has been stylishly remodelled. The interiors are subtle but feature distinctive local South African art. Facilities here include a pamper room and a patio overlooking a pool.

Villa Zest

MAP P2 ∎ 2 Braemar Rd, Green Point ∎ 021 433 1246 ∎ www.villazest. co.za ∎ RR

With suites given names such as Barbarella, Warhol and Xanadu, you know you can expect something a little different here. The interior design is striking – from the eclectic art in the communal areas to the individually designed 1970s-inspired rooms. Excellent service and fabulous breakfasts complete the package.

Peninsula All-Suite Hotel

MAP J4 ∎ 313 Beach Rd, Sea Point ∎ 021 430 7777 ∎ www.peninsula.co.za ∎ RRR

This seafront Art Deco high-rise hotel offers spectacular views and has self-catering apartments. Facilities include a pool and a complimentary shuttle to various sites. The surrounding area has a range of shops ideal for self-caterers. It's understandably popular with families and small groups of friends.

The Three Boutique Hotel

MAP P7 ∎ 3 Flower St, Oranjezicht ∎ 021 465 7517 ∎ www.thethree. co.za ∎ RRR

Historic and modern combine in this boutique hotel housed in a lovely colonnade-fronted building dating back to 1740. Guests can relax in the black-and-white tiled wrap-around verandah or on the pool terrace. There is also a guest tennis court.

Winchester Mansions

MAP L2 ∎ 221 Beach Rd, Sea Point ∎ 021 434 2351 ∎ www.winchester.co.za ∎ RRR

A 1920s building set around a bougainvillea-clad courtyard and right on the promenade at Sea Point. Rooms on the lower floor have a floral Edwardian feel, while those on the upper floors are spacious and modern.

Budget Hotels

Daddy Long Legs

MAP P4 ∎ 134 Long St ∎ 021 422 3074 ∎ www. daddylonglegs.co.za ∎ R

Situated at the heart of the action on Long Street, this bold boutique hotel defies any conventional description. Each one of its 13 rooms has been uniquely, if perhaps rather bizarrely, decorated by different artists.

The New Tulbagh Hotel

MAP Q4 ∎ 9 Ryk Tulbagh Square ∎ 021 418 5161 ∎ www.newtulbaghhotel. com ∎ RR

The 60 simple, spacious rooms at this centrally located hotel are well equipped. Rates include a buffet-style breakfast. There's a cosy bar overlooking the square. It's close to the train and bus stations and also only a short stroll from the V&A Waterfront.

Underberg Guest House

MAP N5 ∎ 6 Tamboerskloof Rd, Tamboerskloof ∎ 021 426 2262 ∎ www. underbergguesthouse. co.za ∎ RR

Set in a pretty location below Table Mountain, this charming nine-room guesthouse was built as a farmhouse in the 1860s and features old-world verandahs and cosy lounges. It is within walking distance from the restaurants on Kloof Street and ideal for exploring the city centre.

Wilton Manor

MAP N2 ■ 15 Croxteth Rd, Green Point ■ 021 434 7869 ■ www.wiltonguest houses.co.za ■ RR

Lying in a quiet corner of Green Point, minutes away from the city centre, this restored Victorian manor has a wraparound balcony, pressed ceilings and wooden floors. Its thatched wooden deck has a heated pool. The seven double rooms can be booked individually or as a block unit.

Southern Suburbs & Peninsula Hotels

Chartfield Guesthouse

MAP H3 ■ 30 Gatesville Rd, Kalk Bay ■ 021 788 3793 ■ www.chartfield. co.za ■ R

This grand old building with 16 modern rooms overlooks Kalk Bay harbour. Shops, a beach and a glut of great restaurants are nearby.

Quayside Hotel

MAP H4 ■ Jubilee Sq, St George's St, Simon's Town ■ 021 786 3838 ■ www.aha.co.za/ quayside ■ RR

Located above the Quayside Centre (see p88), this wallet-friendly four-star hotel has wonderful views. The 26 rooms here are very spacious, but it's well worth paying the slight premium for a sea-facing one with a balcony.

The Andros Deluxe Boutique Hotel

MAP H2 ■ Cnr Newlands & Phyllis rds, Claremont ■ 021 797 9777 ■ www. andros.co.za ■ RRR

This hotel is set in one of the most exclusive

addresses in Cape Town – a 1908 Cape Dutch homestead designed by Sir Herbert Baker. All 15 rooms have verandas and are sumptuously furnished with antiques. There is also a suite with a private pool. Facilities include a gym, beauty salon and a candlelit country restaurant.

The Cellars-Hohenort

MAP H2 ■ 93 Brommers-vlei Rd, Constantia ■ 021 794 2137 ■ www. collectionmcgrath.com ■ RRR

This elegant five-star hotel is set in grounds bordering Kirstenbosch National Botanical Garden. It has a very classy set-up, with a strong period feel and two excellent restaurants, one of which, Greenhouse (see p81), offers fresh, seasonal menus and wine-pairing.

The Last Word Constantia

MAP H2 ■ Spaanschemat River Rd, Constantia ■ 021 794 7657 ■ www. thelastword.co.za ■ RRR

This boutique hotel has four superior doubles and five suites. The interior combines contemporary decor with a scattering of modern African art. The hotel operates primarily as a B&B, but staff can prepare meals on request, or you can explore the nearby dining options.

Steenberg Hotel

MAP H3 ■ Steenberg Estate, Tokai ■ 021 713 2222 ■ www.steenberg farm.com ■ RRR

This intimate five-star hotel on the Steenberg Estate has fine thatched-and-gabled Cape Dutch

architecture. There are two excellent restaurants, Catharina's and Bistro Sixteen82 (see p81), and guests can access the Steenberg Golf Course.

Tintswalo Atlantic

MAP G3 ■ Chapman's Peak Drive, Hout Bay ■ 021 201 0025 ■ http:// tintswalo.com ■ RRR

Hanging over the Atlantic Ocean on Chapman's Peak Drive, this five-star resort boasts one of the best locations of any hotel in Cape Town. The utterly gorgeous suites combine classic decor with modern touches, and reflect the beauty of their natural surroundings. Facilities include a fabulous pool on a wooden deck just metres from the ocean.

Vineyard Hotel

MAP H2 ■ 60 Colinton Rd, Newlands ■ 021 657 4500 ■ www.vineyard. co.za ■ RRR

The Vineyard is centred around a 1799 country manor, set in a lush riverside garden estate, which was built for the Scottish traveller and society hostess Lady Anne Barnard. This luxurious hotel offers a variety of rooms, a quartet of restaurants – including a sushi bar – and two heated swimming pools.

Winelands Town Hotels

Coopmanhuijs Boutique Hotel

MAP D2 ■ 33 Church St, Stellenbosch ■ 021 883 8207 ■ www.coopman huijs.co.za ■ RR

Set within an 18th-century heritage building, the 16 compact rooms at this boutique hotel have plenty of character. Some rooms have good-sized balconies, and there is a charming streetside terrace, where you can sip a glass of local wine while watching the world go by in central Stellenbosch. There is also a pool and Helena's restaurant *(see p98)*.

Akademie Street Boutique Hotel
MAP F2 ▪ 5 Akademie St ▪ Franschhoek ▪ 082 517 0405 ▪ www.aka.co.za ▪ RRR
In a quiet side-street just a short walk from the town centre, Akademie is made up of luxurious suites in various buildings scattered around the garden. Three rooms have their own private pools, while the other three share a larger pool. An incredibly peaceful place to stay.

Batavia Boutique Hotel
MAP D2 ▪ 12 Louw St, Stellenbosch ▪ 021 887 2914 ▪ www.batavia-stellenbosch.co.za ▪ RRR
Experience the grandeur of a classical 19th-century guesthouse, but with all modern conveniences. The Batavia's nine luxurious suites are all individually designed with carefully selected antique and contemporary pieces.

Grande Roche Hotel
MAP E1 ▪ Plantasie St, Paarl ▪ 021 863 5100 ▪ www.granderoche.com ▪ RRR
One of the top hotels in the Winelands, set at the foot of magnificent Paarl Rock, Grande Roche

is built around a lovely Cape Dutch manor, now listed as a national monument. Its 34 suites have wonderful views.

Mont Rochelle
MAP F2 ▪ Dassenberg Rd, Franschhoek ▪ 021 876 2770 ▪ www.virgin limitededition.com/en/ mont-rochelle ▪ RRR
This five-star hotel on the Mont Rochelle Wine Estate offers fabulous views over Franschhoek. Built in the classic Cape Dutch style, it has 26 elegant rooms and suites, two fine restaurants, a spa and a heated outdoor pool.

Oude Werf Hotel
MAP D2 ▪ 30 Church St, Stellenbosch ▪ 021 887 4608 ▪ www.oudewerf hotel.co.za ▪ RRR
Established in 1802 on the foundations of a fire-damaged church, this Stellenbosch institution is South Africa's oldest country inn. It has an atmospheric ambience and a handy location on historic Church Street. It offers 58 rooms and a fine Cape restaurant.

Winelands Rural Hotels

Cascade Manor
MAP E1 ▪ Waterval Rd, Nederburg, Paarl ▪ 021 868 0227 ▪ www.cascade manor.co.za ▪ RR
Perched at the end of a gravel road some 10 km (6 miles) outside of Paarl, Cascade Manor is named for the small waterfall found at the end of a path cutting through the olive grove. Rooms edge the manicured lawns, with terraces looking out onto the pool area.

Eikendal Lodge
MAP D3 ▪ R44 south of Stellenbosch ▪ 021 855 3617 ▪ www.eiken dallodge.co.za ▪ RR
This vine-draped lodge is set among the Eikendal Estate vineyards. There is an excellent Italian restaurant, and facilities include a fly-fishing clinic as well as plenty of other outdoor activities.

Kleine Zalze Lodge
MAP D3 ▪ R44, Stellenbosch ▪ 021 880 0740 ▪ www.kleine zalze.co.za ▪ RR
This lodge offers four-star accommodation (with the option for self-catering) close to Stellenbosch. It is set among oak trees with mountain and golf-course views. Its Terroir restaurant *(see p98)* is an acclaimed destination for lovers of fine food.

Spier Hotel
MAP D3 ▪ Spier Wine Farm, R310, Stellenbosch ▪ 021 809 1100 ▪ www.spier.co.za ▪ RR
This four-star hotel overlooks the Eerste River on Spier Farm, a short drive from Stellenbosch. The 153 contemporary rooms are arranged around six courtyards. It also has a pool.

WedgeView Country House & Spa
MAP D3 ▪ Bonniemile Rd, Stellenbosch ▪ 021 881 3525 ▪ www.wedge view.co.za ▪ RR
Indulge in five-star luxury at this private country residence with 18 individually decorated rooms, heated pools and a spa. There are magnificent views of the surrounding vineyards.

For a key to hotel price categories see p114

Asara Wine Farm

MAP D3 ■ Polkadraai Rd,
Stellenbosch ■ 021 888
8000 ■ www.asara.co.za
■ RRR

With 40 rooms, this is one
of the larger hotels in the
Winelands and offers fine
views and wine tasting –
the latter within walking
distance of your room.
There's a pool, three restaurants, spa treatments
and a walking trail laid
out through the vineyards.

The Devon
Valley Hotel

MAP D2 ■ Devon Valley
Rd, near Stellenbosch
■ 021 865 2012 ■ www.
devonvalleyhotel.com
■ RRR

Set on the Sylvanvale
Estate, this popular, four-
star country retreat offers
lovely views and retains an
elegant Edwardian feel.
Guests can stroll through
the surrounding vineyards
or dine in the award-win-
ning Flavours Restaurant.

Lanzerac

MAP E3 ■ 1 Lanzerac Rd,
Stellenbosch ■ 021 887
1132 ■ www.lanzerac.
co.za ■ RRR

This prestigious hotel is
centred on a handsome
300-year-old Cape Dutch
estate. Equipped with five-
star facilities including a
spa, the whole set-up
positively exudes luxury.

The Light House

MAP E1 ■ 2 Lille St,
Courtrai, Paarl ■ 021 873
4600 ■ http://thelight
house.co.za ■ RRR

Expect tip-top service at
this boutique guesthouse,
set amid vineyards. The
five large suites boast
sumptuous decor and
overlook the expansive
gardens and pool.

La Petite Ferme

MAP F2 ■ Franschhoek
Pass Rd, Franschhoek
■ 021 876 3016■ www.
lapetiteferme.co.za ■ RRR

The view over the entire
Franschhoek wine valley
from these suites and
self-catering cottages is
mesmerizing. There's a
well-regarded restaurant
(see p99) and intimate
winery, so you can eat
and drink in style.

Le Quartier Français

MAP F2 ■ Wilhelmina &
Berg sts, Franschhoek
■ 021 876 2151 ■ www.
leeucollection.com/lqf
■ RRR

This legendary five-star
hotel offers 21 rooms and
suites around the rose-
filled courtyard and the
swimming pool; each has
lounges and artworks
by local artists. It is also
highly acclaimed for its
restaurant, The Tasting
Room (see pp58 & 99).

Hotels Beyond
the Winelands

Farr Out Guesthouse

MAP S2 ■ 17 Seemeeus-
ingel, Paternoster ■ 022
752 2222 ■ www.farrout.
co.za ■ R

This four-room establish-
ment on the outskirts of
Paternoster offers a rustic
but plush wigwam tent
in the *fynbos* field. Two of
the rooms have balconies
with sea views. It is the
perfect place to enjoy
the wonderful natural
sights of Cape Columbine.

Old Mac Daddy
Luxury Trailer Park

MAP F4 ■ Valley Rd, Elgin
■ 021 884 0241 ■ www.
oldmacdaddy.co.za ■ R

Long, sleek Airstream
trailers were imported
from the US to create this
part-caravan-park/part-
designer-farm resort.
Each of the iconic vehicles
has been decorated by
an artist in über-modern,
often outrageous themes.
This charmingly eccentric
place is about an hour's
drive east of Cape Town.

Agulhas
Country Lodge

MAP V6 ■ Main Rd,
L'Agulhas ■ 028 435 7650
■ www.agulhascountry
lodge.com ■ RR

Set on a hill overlooking
the southernmost point
in Africa, this family-run
guesthouse offers just
eight rooms, all with great
views. The lodge's fine-
dining restaurant serves
some of the best seafood
on the south coast.

Misty Waves
Boutique Hotel

MAP U5 ■ 21 Marine Dr,
Hermanus ■ 028 313
8460 ■ www.hermanus
mistybeach.co.za ■ RR

A curvaceous building
on the cliffs, with a
lounge, pool, private
Jacuzzi and a great sea-
food restaurant with
stunning views across
the bay. It's also an
excellent place for
whale watching.

Robertson
Small Hotel

MAP V4 ■ 58 Van
Reenen St, Robertson
■ 023 626 7200 ■ www.
therobertsonsmallhotel.
com ■ RR

This grand Victorian
home offers the smartest
accommodation in town
and has a fine in-house
restaurant. The sleepy
valley of wine and olives
is a popular weekend
escape from Cape Town.

Abalone Guest Lodge

MAP U5 ▪ 306 Main Rd, Hermanus ▪ 044 533 1345 ▪ www.abalone lodge.co.za ▪ RRR

Situated on Sievers Point, this pleasantly decorated guesthouse is ideal for cliff walks, superb land-based whale watching and exploring the small town centre of Hermanus.

Cliff Lodge

MAP U6 ▪ 6 Cliff St, De Kelders, Gansbaai ▪ 028 384 0983 ▪ www. clifflodge.co.za ▪ RRR

Located on a magnificent clifftop outside Gansbaai, this award-winning place offers spectacular views of Walker Bay, and consists of four spacious rooms and a suite. There's also a shared conservatory and deck with ocean views, and a plunge pool.

The Marine Hermanus

MAP U5 ▪ Marine Dr, Hermanus ▪ 028 313 1000 ▪ www.collection mcgrath.com ▪ RRR

The very best address in Hermanus offers accommodation in rooms and suites. The patio is a vantage point for whale watching, and facilities include a spa, tidal pool and two great restaurants.

Backpacker Hostels

Ashanti Lodge

MAP P6 ▪ 11 Hof St, Gardens ▪ 021 423 8721 ▪ Breakfast excl ▪ www. ashanti.co.za ▪ R

Combining upmarket decor with a relaxed party atmosphere, this place serves meals and drinks in the bar. The deck has views of Table Mountain.

The Backpack

MAP N5 ▪ 74 New Church St, Tamboerskloof ▪ 021 423 4530 ▪ Breakfast excl ▪ www.back packers.co.za ▪ R

One of South Africa's oldest backpacker hostels, this place offers luxurious rooms along with the standard dorms. It has a very experienced travel centre that can help you with your excursion plans.

Hermanus Backpackers

MAP U5 ▪ 26 Flower St, Hermanus ▪ 028 312 4293 ▪ www.backpackers. thebuzz.co.za ▪ R

This lively hostel has a range of accommodation, from dorms to a self-contained cottages, and offers activities ranging from caged shark dives at Gansbaai to cliff walks, whale watching and wine tasting along the Walker Bay wine route.

Long Street Backpackers

MAP P5 ▪ 209 Long St ▪ 021 423 0615 ▪ Breakfast excl ▪ www.long streetbackpackers.com ▪ R

The oldest and probably the best backpacker hostel along Long Street, within easy reach of the trendy nightspots. It's a secure, friendly and lively place for those who want to be at the heart of the urban action.

Otter's Bend Lodge

MAP F2 ▪ Dassenberg Rd, Franschhoek ▪ 021 876 3200 ▪ Breakfast excl ▪ www.ottersbendlodge. co.za ▪ R

This budget hostel fills a gap in Franschhoek's accommodation scene, and it's in a pretty location. There's a dorm, three en-suite rooms and two cabins that sleep up to four people. Otter's Bend Lodge also arranges outdoor activities for guests.

St John's Waterfront Lodge

MAP P2 ▪ 6 Braemar Rd, Green Pt ▪ 021 439 1404 ▪ Breakfast excl ▪ www. stjohns.co.za ▪ R

Set in the suburb of Green Point, this welcoming and well-established hostel offers rooms and dorms and is a short walk (not advisable late at night) from the V&A Waterfront and a bus ride from the city.

Sea Shack

MAP S2 ▪ Cape Columbine Nature Reserve, Paternoster ▪ 079 820 6824 ▪ Breakfast excl ▪ www.seashack.co.za ▪ R

The ultimate backpacker hostel for outdoor enthusiasts. The Sea Shack offers simple accommodation in tents and wooden cabins. Other attractions include guided sea kayaking, boat trips, snorkelling and lovely walks through the reserve and on the sandy beaches. The power provided is solar or gas.

Stumble Inn

MAP D2 ▪ 12 Market St, Stellenbosch ▪ 021 887 4049 ▪ Breakfast excl ▪ www.stumbleinn backpackers.co.za ▪ R

Stumble Inn is located close to historic Dorp Street, and is thus very convenient for exploring the Stellenbosch CBD. Facilities include a swimming pool and a TV lounge.

General Index

Acknowledgments

Author
Born in Britain and raised in Johannesburg, Philip Briggs is the author of more than a dozen travel guides about Africa. He is also a regular contributor to magazines such as *Travel Africa*, *Africa Geographic*, *Wanderlust* and *BBC Wildlife*

Additional contributor
Lucy Corne

Publishing Director Georgina Dee

Publisher Vivien Antwi

Design Director Phil Ormerod

Editorial Sophie Adam, Ankita Awasthi Tröger, Michelle Crane, Rachel Fox, Fay Franklin, Alison McGill, Sally Schafer, Hollie Teague

Cover Design Richard Czapnik

Design Hansa Babra, Tessa Bindloss, Bharti Karakoti, Rahul Kumar, Bhavika Mathur, Ankita Sharma, Stuti Tiwari, Vinita Venugopal

Picture Research Subhadeep Biswas, Taiyaba Khatoon, Ellen Root, Rituraj Singh

Cartography Zafar ul Islam Khan, Suresh Kumar, James Macdonald, Casper Morris

DTP Jason Little

Production Luca Bazzoli

Factchecker Lizzie Williams

Proofreader Clare Peel

Indexer Helen Peters

First edition created by Quadrum Solutions, Mumbai

Picture Credits
The publisher would like to thank the following for their kind permission to reproduce their photographs:

Key: a-above; b-below/bottom; c-centre; f-far; l-left; r-right; t-top

123RF.com: Patrick Burn LPSSA 62cb; Grobler du Preez 47br; Eric Reisenberger 48c; Leonardo Spencer 51tl.

Alamy Stock Photo: ASK Images 67tr; Pocholo Calapre 86–7; Harry Eggens 11tl; epa european pressphoto agency b.v. 44tr; Greg Balfour Evans 21crb, 35br; Tony French 4t; joan gravell 34cl; Greatstock 17crb; Hemis 18–19, 19tc, 103cl; hemis.fr / René Mattes 57t; imageBROKER 2tr, 38–9; INTERFOTO 3tl, 4cl, 64–5; Frans Lemmens 52tl; Angus McComiskey 11crb; Eric Nathan 13cr, 28–9, 34–5, 63clb; National Geographic Creative 16bl; NSP-RF 1; Blaize Pascall 56clb; Juergen Ritterbach 6cl; RosalreneBetancourt 8 42t; willie sator 36t; Peter Schickert 4cla; Erik Schlogl 4cr; M. Sobreira 15crb, 78tl; Antony Souter 10cla, 18cla, 18br, 21tl, 21c, 29crb, 31tl; Pete Titmuss 14cl; Peter Titmuss 26cl; Ann and Steve Toon 102t; Travel Pictures 24–5; travelstock44 4clb; Ariadne Van Zandbergen 35tc, 42bl, 43tr, 74t, 85br, 101b, 102clb; Jeffrey Zane 53br.

AWL Images: Aurora Photos 54–5; Danita Delimont Stock 22cl, 86cr; Michele Falzone 10c, 91t; Ian Trower 70cra.

Babel at Babylonstoren: 98cb.

Bascule Whisky and Wine Bar: 73t.

Bistro Sixteen82: 81cra.

Blue Train Park: 56br.

Boschendal Wine Estate: 92clb.

Burgundy Restaurant: 105cr.

Culture Club: Claire Gunn 77cb.

Dreamstime.com: Agaliza 50cr; Andrew Allport 23tl; Bennymarty 69cl; Neil Bradfield 31cr; Bradleyvdw 32–3; Pocholo Calapre 46b, 68b; Lenise Calleja 49cra; Cncphotographylee 55tl; Richard Cooksey 17tl; Neal Cooper 84cla; Delstudio 48t; Ecophoto 26–7; Maria Luisa Lopez Estivill 44cclb, 80t, 100tl; Mitchell Gunn 54cla; Jaysi 33cr; Leonardospencer 43cl; Danil Lugovoi 30–31; Maurizio De Mattei 33br; Guilherme Gomes De Mesquita 16–17c; Micoppiens 59br; Alexander Mychko 59tr; Nomisg 53c; Photogallet 101cr; Photosky 10–11, 50b; Marek Poplawski 85t; Grobler Du Preez 10bl, 12–13, 13br, 20bl, 26bl, 30bl, 33tl, 75b, 92br; Luca Roggero 45b; Himanshu Saraf 11cr; Sculpies 22–3; Sohadiszno 86tl; David Steele 11cra, 79b; Joshua Wanyama 14–15; Andrea Willmore 66ca; Hongqi Zhang (aka Michael Zhang) 72cla; Kostiantyn Zloschastiev 90cla, 93tl, 104tr.

Ethno Bongo: 88bl.

Franschhoek Motor Museum: 36c.

Getty Images: Jenny Acheson 51br; Peter Adams 4crb; Shaen Adey 14br, 29tl; Denny Allen 10clb; Stephen Alvarez 23cl; Heinrich van den Berg 40c; Bloomberg 28clb; Peter Chadwick 16cl; DEA Picture Library 40b; Danita Delimont 30crb; Nigel Dennis 46tl; Ulrich Doering 47cl; Education Images 20–21, 61tr; Thierry Falise 72crb; Gallo Images 63tr; Blaine Harrington III 7br, 11br; Mark Harris 34br; Jon Hicks 4b; Samir Hussein 41tr; Alexander Joe 41cl; John Lamb 80br; Lonely Planet 77cra; Yasir Nisar 60b; Kazuhiro Nogi 55br; Neil Overy 104b; Peter Pinnock 53tl; Rhapsode 29c; Merten Snijders 61cl, 67br,

68cla, 70bl; Ruby Soho 37tr; Tier Und Naturfotografie J und C Sohns 32br; The Times / Shelley Christians 91br; Richard du Toit 79tr; David Wall Photo 71ca; Carl Warner 52b,;Ariadne Van Zandbergen 12bl.

Grande Provence Restaurant: 99cr.

Harbour House: 76br, 89clb.

iStockphoto.com: Agnieszka Gaul 3tr, 82–3, 106–7; Jan-Otto 49b; shumski 2tl, 8–9.

Karoo Classics: 94clb.

Kirstenbosch National Botanical Garden: 26tl, 27crb; *Bringing Condolences* by Norbert Shamyarira. 27tc.

Kleine Zalze: Terroir 58br.

La Motte: 37cl, 96tl.

Meerlust: 97crb.

Oranjezicht City Farm: Coco van Oppens 60tl.

Quagga Rare Books & Art: 88tr.

Le Quartier Francais: 58t.

Rex Shutterstock: Gallo Images 62t.

Root 44 Market: 94ca.

Savoy Cabbage: 59cl.

Sevruga: 76tl.

Spier Wine Farm: 57cr, 61br.

Tokara: 95b, 98cla.

Woodstock Exchange: 71crb.

Cover

Front and spine: **4Corners:** Richard Taylor

Back: **Dreamstime.com:** Herrbullermann

Pull Out Map Cover

4Corners: Richard Taylor

All other images © Dorling Kindersley

For further information see: www.dkimages.com

Penguin
Random
House

Printed and bound in China

First published in Great Britain in 2008 by Dorling Kindersley Limited 80 Strand, London WC2R 0RL

Copyright 2008, 2017 © Dorling Kindersley Limited

A Penguin Random House Company

17 18 19 20 10 9 8 7 6 5 4 3 2

Reprinted with revisions 2010, 2014, 2017

A CIP catalogue record is available from the British Library.

ISBN 978 0 2412 7869 7

MIX
Paper from responsible sources
FSC™ C018179

SPECIAL EDITIONS OF DK TRAVEL GUIDES

DK Travel Guides can be purchased in bulk quantities at discounted prices for use in promotions or as premiums. We are also able to offer special editions and personalized jackets, corporate imprints, and excerpts from all of our books, tailored specifically to meet your own needs.

To find out more, please contact:

in the US
specialsales@dk.com

in the UK
travelguides@uk.dk.com

in Canada
specialmarkets@dk.com

in Australia
penguincorporatesales@ penguinrandomhouse.com.au

As a guide to abbreviations in the visitor information blocks: **Adm** = admission charge; **DA** = disabled access.

Selected Street and Towns Index